THE COMMERCIAL LIFE OF A SUFFOLK TO...

Further details of Poppyland Publishing titles can be found at
www.poppyland.co.uk
where clicking on the 'Support and Resources' button
will lead to pages specially compiled to support this book

Framlingham in April 2004: the commercial centre of the town remains largely as it was in 1900, though the town has expanded around it.

The Commercial Life of a Suffolk Town

Framlingham around 1900

John F. Bridges

Victorian pillar box in Double Street – see page 82

POPPYLAND PUBLISHING

Copyright © 2007 John F. Bridges

ISBN 978 0 946148 80 6

Published by Poppyland Publishing, Cromer NR27 9AN

Designed and typeset in 10½ on 12 pt ITC Bodoni Twelve by Watermark, Cromer NR27 9HL

Printed by Barnwell's, Aylsham

Picture credits

Illustrative material has kindly been lent by the following:

Stanley Baines: page 107

Barclays Bank Group Archive: pages 47, 48 (bottom), 49

Betty Berry: pages 54, 82

James Breese Collection: pages 11, 14, 15, 16, 17, 18, 23, 26, 30 (bottom), 33, 37, 40, 42, 45 (top), 46 (bottom), 48 (top), 52, 53, 56 (left), 59, 62 (left), 64, 67 (left), 69, 70, 72 (right), 73 (left), 77 (top), 89, 90 (left), 96 (right), 97 (right), 102, 106 (right), 110 (bottom), 111, 113 (top), 114, 116 (top two), 119, 121 (bottom two), 124, 125, 130 (right), 131 (right), 133, 135 (right), 142 (left), 143, 145 (top & left), 148, 150, 153, 154 (left), 155 (left), 158, 160, 161

BT Archives: pages 84, 85

Phyllis Cockburn: page 128 (right)

Ivan Codd: page 101

John Durrant: page 66

Bill Flemming: page 78

Framlingham Museum: pages 44 (left), 46 (top), 57, 61 (bottom), 90 (right), 145 (bottom right)

Jo Gregory: pages 10, 151

Diana Howard: page 108

Ray Hubbard: pages 34, 35

Ipswich Transport Museum: pages 75, 147 (left)

Dave Kindred: pages 32, 50 (left), 60 (right), 63 (left), 65 (left), 72 (left), 86 (top), 95, 106 (top left), 127, 134, 140, 149

Long Shop Museum, Leiston: page 21

Tony Martin: pages 152, 154 (right)

Mary Moore: page 50 (right)

Tony Moore: page 13

Arthur Newson: pages 41, 58 (bottom), 60 (left), 76

Doreen Nicholls: page 13

Poppyland Photos: page 2

Nic Portway: pages 27, 157

Sudbury Museum Trust: page 19

Suffolk Photographic Survey, Suffolk Record Office: pages 39, 51, 67 (right), 71, 73 (right), 88, 90, 94 (right), 104, 122 (top), 155 (right)

Mary Webster: page 106 (bottom left)

Steve Williams: pages 43, 44 (right), 81 (top), 120

All other material is from the author's collection.

Foreword

Until the great changes that occurred following the First World War almost all towns and a good many of the larger villages were to a great extent self supporting. Country dwellers could find almost all they needed in the nearest market town, where a variety of shops sold meat, groceries, bread and confectionery, fish, clothes, shoes, china and glass, furniture, and indeed everything a shopper might require. Tradesmen from the humble boot and shoemaker to the blacksmith, from the plumber to the machinist and cycle agent, and from the carpenter to the miller were to be found in almost every community, and the farmer wanting a new wagon or tumbrel did not have to go far to find a craftsman who could produce just what he wanted.

Small wonder that many country people regarded a visit to the county town as a special event; they had little cause to go so far as Ipswich or Bury St Edmunds when their market town, a mere few miles away, could supply all that they needed. If some-thing so exotic that it was not stocked in one of the local shops was demanded, the local carrier would take the order to Ipswich, whose shopkeepers boasted that they obtained their choicest stock from London, and the required article would be available by the next market day. What changes have come to the countryside! Almost every family has a car, and the family's food requirements can all be acquired in a single visit to the supermarket, which can also supply articles of ready-made clothing, DVDs for home entertainment and much else that was never dreamed of by the housewife traipsing round the shops of Framlingham a hundred years or so ago. With the coming of the supermarket the specialist shops of the old market towns and the general shops of the villages have put up their shutters and faded into history. The craftsmen, too, have deserted their workshops and retired to the churchyard.

The picture that John Bridges paints is of a market town, Framlingham, towards the end of this era of self sufficiency. He grants us a chance to glimpse what George Ewart Evans called the prior culture. It is easy to look back and talk of 'the good old days', but we should resist the temptation to do so. There was much that was satisfying about those times, particularly for those who were sufficiently wealthy to enjoy the good things of life, but there were many in the Suffolk countryside who found the work hard and life in poverty even harder.

The fact that local history groups and societies are springing up in so many towns and villages and that so many people are taking an interest in the not-too-distant past shows that there is a strong feeling of nostalgia for that pre-supermarket culture and the country life that has passed away. This book will prove a popular and welcome addition to the literature of Suffolk.

Robert Malster
2006

Jarvis Scoggins' shop was opposite the White Horse Inn. It had been described as 'Little Whiteleys', in reference to the large London department store. He stocked a vast range of goods including beds, clothing, shoes, furniture and wallpaper. People did not usually need to look beyond the local town to fulfil their shopping needs.

Acknowledgements

There are many people who have helped me in the research for this book. Each subject has its special knowledge or custom that was known only to those who were closely involved with it. I have been most fortunate in obtaining guidance from several specialists in those fields, and hope they will forgive me for condensing their experiences into these small sections.

I would like to thank the following: Stanley Baines, Jim and Betty Berry, Chris Bowden, Stuart Bowell, Mary Brackenbury, Jim and Joan Breese, Dr E. M. Bridges, David Burnett, Ivan and Jan Carter, Geoffrey Clarke, Peter Clarke, Roger Clark, Dr E. E. Cockayne, Phyllis Cockburn, Hugh Coryn, John and Thelma Durrant, John Felgate, Bill Flemming, Tony Flick, Brian Flint, Jo Gregory, Richard Hayes, Barbara Holt, Diana Howard, Martin Howard, Ray Hubbard, Christopher Jay, Muriel Kilvert, David Kindred, Gus Kitson, John Maulden, John McEwan, Peter Minter, Tony Moore, Arthur Newson, Ray and Doreen Nicholls, Graham Pattrick, Alison Pickup, Rev. Canon David Pitcher, Nic Portway, Philip Ryder-Davies, Brian Seward, Pat Sharps, John Symonds, John Simpson, Gordon Sly, Bill Vincent, Sydney Vice and Steve Williams.

Also to Barclays Bank Group Archives, Larysa Bolton; BT Group Archives; Fram Fare, Stephanie Bennell; Ipswich Transport Museum, Brian Dyes; National Gas Archives; The Long Shop Museum, Stephen Mael; The Maltsters Association of Great Britain, Ivor Murrell; Museum of English Rural Life, Reading University, Dr Brown; Suffolk Horse Society, Chris Miller; Suffolk Record Office, Bridget Hanley.

A special thank you to Gill Buckles and Annette Hunter for reading my handwriting and preparing numerous drafts of the text. Also to my wife Pat for producing the artwork for the front cover.

Tony Martin has encouraged me throughout, and I have enjoyed our long telephone conversations trying to resolve such issues as the weight of a sack of beans or the type of wood used in cart axles.

I am pleased to include work by my friend the late John Western. He captured in exquisite detail many aspects of the old buildings and ways of life in Suffolk, leaving us with an important legacy for future generations.

I would also like to acknowledge the work of those earlier writers who had the foresight to record so much of the disappearing way of life in the country. Robert Malster has written many books covering various aspects of the history of our eastern counties. I was therefore delighted and honoured when he agreed to write a foreword for this book. Thanks, Bob.

Finally, to anyone I have inadvertently forgotten, a big thank you also.

John F. Bridges
Little Waldingfield,
Suffolk.
2006

Contents

Framlingham businessmen photographed at the rear of the Crown Hotel at the time of the 1931 Pageant. REAR, LEFT TO RIGHT: *Hubert Ling, solicitor; Donald Clarke, farmer; Walter Fairweather, garage owner; Hugh Clarke, farmer and corn merchant; Mr Warren, headmaster; Frank Rochfort Garrard* JP; *John Self junior, tailor; Harry Maulden, printer; A. G. Potter, Ford agent; Percy Stannard, solicitor's clerk.* FRONT, LEFT TO RIGHT: *Bernard Cossons, Barclays bank manager; George Summers, sub postmaster; Alfred Pretty, retired College master; William Brunger, secretary to College; John Booth; Channing Dowsing, tailor; Thomas Wright, piano tuner; Chris Simmons, general dealer. (John Booth was an Old Framlinghamian, who wrote a number of books including* Framlingham College: The First Sixty Years *and a treatise on Nicholas Danforth, the Framlingham yeoman who sailed to America in 1635.)*

Introduction

The period around 1900 forms the basis for this book. It reflects the beginning of a century which would see great changes in our lives and established patterns of work. I have at times strayed several years either side of this date, but it has not been my intention to record the many changes that occurred throughout the twentieth century. Let us hope that someone will be inspired to do so.

The aim has been to provide a short description of typical commercial activities in a small Suffolk town, along with local examples. It is not possible to do justice to many of the subjects, as several would merit a book on their own account.

Framlingham is the focus for the book, mainly due to my personal connections with the town and access to specific archive material, but the picture was similar in other places of comparable population. My five times great grandfather, Silvanus Bridges, came to Framlingham about 1724 and set up as a blacksmith in Double Street, with his descendants carrying on the trade into the twentieth century. They married into other business families. Richard Green, the author and printer, was brother in law to John Fruer Bridges. The Fruer family were involved in much of the building work in the town, and that name was adopted through marriage.

It is the main trades, professions and services that have been covered, but there were many others such as the basket maker, chimney sweep, hairdresser, jeweller, ropemaker and thatcher. Also, many trades overlapped, with the corn merchant sometimes being a maltster as well as a coal merchant. Even more confusing, the grocer might also be a draper. The wide range of people involved with clothing and furnishings is covered under drapers and outfitters, but also includes dressmakers, milliners and tailors, whose combined numbers represented 10% of the work force.

There were often several people in the same trade, who can be identified from the 1900 commercial directory in Appendix 1. A map is provided to locate business premises near the centre of Framlingham which are referred to in the text. The currency of the time, along with other measurements, will not be familiar to future generations, and appropriate conversion factors are provided in Appendix 5. A list of places to visit is included as Appendix 6.

The concept for this book had been with me for a long time. Tony Martin also has a lifelong interest in the history of Framlingham, and had suggested to me on several occasions that it was time for a new book on the subject. It was his persistence, along with the James Breese material, that finally moved the project along.

James Heffer, thatcher, lived in Station Road. He is holding the yoke which was used to carry the straw onto the roof. The bundle contains hazel sticks, called broaches, which were twisted into the shape of a staple and driven into the thatch.

William 'Sonny' Moore (second left), in the doorway of his barber's shop in Crown and Anchor Lane, 1910. The pole fixed to the wall related back to an earlier age when the barber would also act as a surgeon. Blood letting had been a common practice, with the red and white stripes on the pole representing bandages.

Photographs of people at work are an essential part of this book, and these have been drawn from towns and villages across the county, and combined with the accounts to portray the commercial life of the time. Where necessary, material from a different period and location has been used, in order to illustrate a specific activity.

My childhood was spent in Framlingham in the 1950s, with much of it around the castle and the meres. I do recall that Howard the harnessmaker, Asher Symonds the boot repairer, Simpson the baker and other traditional trades were still in business. At harvest time, the combine was a common sight, but the reaper binder was still used, and I remember helping to gather the sheaves into shocks at Grange Farm. The fondest memory I have is of Ernie Levett, the last blacksmith who worked in the Fairfield Road forge. He seemed to me a kind giant of a man, who could neither read nor write, but explained with great patience various aspects of the blacksmith's trade. The sight, sound and smell of the hot shoeing of Suffolk horses left a great impression on me. I now know that I was witnessing the dying stages of a trade that had endured for centuries.

Ernie Levett

The James Breese Collection

James Breese was born in 1861 and was one of five boys brought up on their father's farm at Benningham Hall, Occold. He went to Framlingham College in 1874, and later became involved with the farm, looking after the stock and the horses. By raising pigs he was able to save £400, a large sum of money for a man of only 23. He then decided it was time to hire a nearby farm. Good advice at the time reckoned that you shouldn't go far looking for a farm or a wife. James was well aware of the need for hard work, and eventually took on another farm in order to be more profitable. Over time he bought further land and two more farms, bringing his total acreage to over a thousand. However, he reckoned to make no real money from farming until the outbreak of war in 1914, and before that never made more than an average of £1 a coomb for corn.

James lived at Church Farm, Saxtead, which he rented from S. G. Carley from 1889 until he purchased it in 1914. The annual rent in 1900 was £120. With the assistance of his eldest son Norton, he also farmed at World's End, Saxtead. His younger sons, Herbert and Alfred, farmed White Hall, Debenham, and Grove Farm, Ashfield cum Thorpe, respectively. James died in 1944 at the age of 82.

RIGHT: *James Breese with his son Herbert at Church Farm, Saxtead.*

James Breese ready to plough with a pair of Suffolk horses.

His approach to farming was very much that of a business, which was somewhat unusual at the time, but essential in that period of long depression and low prices. Keeping a record of income and expenditure would be an important part of that process.

I visited his son Alfred when he was living in retirement. He showed me a few old bills, one of which was for my great grandfather's blacksmith shop. On leaving, he mentioned that his son Jim had sev-eral more, and I might like to see him also. I made a note to contact him, but time passed on and sadly so did Alfred, before I made that visit.

I will never forget the day when, with my wife Pat, we visited Jim and Joan Breese. They went off to collect the material from a shed in the garden. After several trips with the wheelbarrow, seven large black bin liners were deposited on the floor, each bulging with paperwork. As the Breese family lived in the Saxtead area, much of their trade was

RAT AND RABBIT CATCHERS

_ Mr. J. Breese.

Dr. TO **WOLTON** BROS.

DATE	DESCRIPTION.	£.	s.	d
6th aug.	3 rats from Church Farm	.	.	6
6th aug.	32 rats from Hill Farm	.	5	4
8th aug.	5 rats from Hill Farm	.	.	10
1st. Sept.	6 rats from Hill Farm	.	1	0
11th Sept.	1 rat from World's End	.	.	2
21st. Sept.	1 rat from Hill Farm	.	.	2
		.	8	0
TOTAL	48 rats			

Paid With
Sept 22nd thanks

FERRET KEEPERS.
R.W.
H.W.

A hand written and illustrated bill for rat catching.

with Framlingham, and the material turned out to be a real treasure trove relating to those early businesses. The original accounts had been put on a spike which, when full, was thrown into the loft. They cover a period from 1882 to 1957. The normal account of that time states 'Dr. to', or 'Bought of', the former meaning debtor. For Framlingham alone, there are over 4,200 bills covering 165 different businesses. This represents only about a third of all the material, with many others in Suffolk for well known names, such as Garrett and Ransome, along with millwrights and photographers etc., which are yet to be catalogued. The discovery of this amazing source has allowed this book to be illustrated by relevant documents. We are fortunate that it was not destroyed at any time over the last 60 years or so.

James also kept records of the wages paid to his men, along with notes of their daily tasks. This material, along with general farming records and many auction catalogues, is lodged with the Suffolk Horse Society, Market Hill, Woodbridge.

One piece of James' advice we men should never forget is, 'Whatever you do, don't go humbuggin' about, whist drivin', and dancing, and don't marry the girl who can't make a dumpling.'

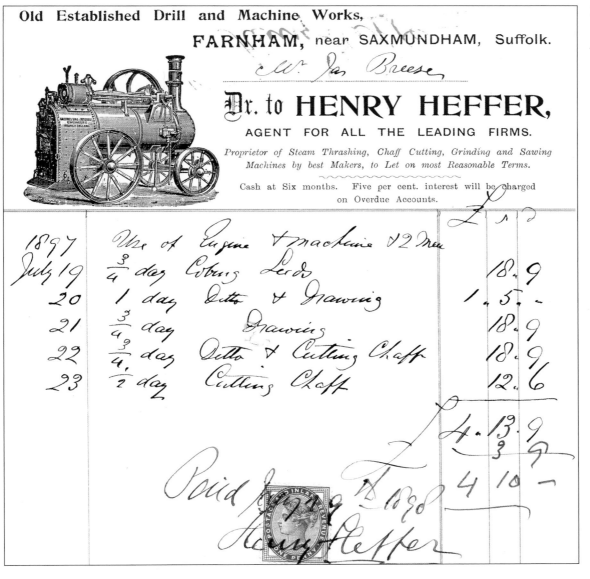

Old Established Drill and Machine Works,
FARNHAM, near SAXMUNDHAM, Suffolk.

Mr Jas Breese

Dr. to HENRY HEFFER,

AGENT FOR ALL THE LEADING FIRMS.

Proprietor of Steam Thrashing, Chaff Cutting, Grinding and Sawing Machines by best Makers, to Let on most Reasonable Terms.

Cash at Six months.   Five per cent. interest will be charged on Overdue Accounts.

1897	Use of Engine & machine & 2 men	£	s	d
July 19	¾ day Coking Leeds		18	9
20	1 day Ditto & Drawing	1	5	-
21	¾ day Drawing		18	9
22	¾ day Ditto & Cutting Chaff		18	9
23	½ day Cutting Chaff		12	6
		4	13	9
		4	10	-

Paid ... 1898   Henry Heffer

Mr Garford the castrator – not an obvious career choice today!

RIGHT: *Jesse Wightman was apprentice to Mr Aldred, the Saxtead miller, before becoming a millwright. The reference to 'secondhand damsell' relates to the iron spindle used with underdrift stones, which taps against a block of wood to shake the grain towards the millstones. It was so called because it made the most noise in the mill.*

The Commercial Life of Framlingham

The prosperity of a market town depends very much on the good fortune of those who patronise its services. When agriculture prospered, there was a similar effect on local trade, but this was not the case for the last quarter of the nineteenth century, and our period around 1900 has to be viewed against the earlier conditions.

Farming generally prospered in the early 1800s when prices were kept high by the Napoleonic war. Fear of falling prices after the war saw the introduction of the Corn Laws in 1815, which prevented foreign imports until corn costs reached a certain level. This was good for agriculture, but disastrous for those on low wages or unemployed. Strong protest, particularly from urban areas, eventually saw the law modified, and then repealed in 1846.

RIGHT: Corn exchanges were built in many towns in the mid-nineteenth century. This fine example in Sudbury dates from 1841. Fortunately, it survives as the library, having been threatened with demolition in the 1960s.

Although this potentially allowed greater imports, the large overseas markets were not yet fully developed, which helped the home market.

The census data for small Suffolk towns, which would include a number of farms (Framlingham

had 25 farms in the 1901 census), show a general increase in population from 1800 to about 1850. Numbers then remain fairly static or decline throughout the second half of the century. Typical population variations are shown in Appendix 2, where the initial decline for Framlingham was offset by the additional staff and pupils of the Albert Memorial College, which opened in 1865. The slow decline was evident in other small towns such as Bungay, Eye, Hadleigh, Halesworth and Mildenhall, while Stradbroke's population in 1901 was even less than in 1801.

It is appropriate to consider whether Framlingham was a broadly typical inland market town. A number are listed in Appendix 2, where the average population was approximately 3,700, against 2,526 for Framlingham. The typical trades such as baker, carpenter and saddler were present in all the towns.

Larger commercial activities have also been evaluated, such as banks, breweries, brickworks, corn exchange, factories, gas works, maltings, local newspaper and railways. These were all represented in Framlingham in 1900, with the exception of any significant factory or works.

These towns all had banks, but some were only open for limited hours. Except for Stradbroke, they all had a gas works and railway, although the Mid Suffolk Light Railway did reach there in 1904.

Maltings were found in most towns and especially in Stowmarket and Halesworth. The malting trade was dying in Framlingham by 1900 as it only served local demand in small quantities, but conversely the corn trade was growing, with E. G. Clarke eventually becoming the largest barley merchant in East Anglia. Brickworks, breweries and corn exchanges were present in most, but not all, towns. Some were also on navigable rivers, for example Bungay, Beccles, Mildenhall, Stowmarket and Sudbury. This was of considerable benefit to trade in earlier times, and had attracted development in the form of granaries and maltings. However, by 1900 the transport of inland goods by water had been long eclipsed by the coming of the railway. The Stour Navigation was in liquidation by 1913, while Stowmarket only saw the occasional barge, and its navigation was officially closed in 1922.

Framlingham was therefore fairly typical of the smaller towns, having most facilities apart from large works or factories. These were found in the larger towns: Gurteen's clothing factory in Haverhill, Clay's printing works in Bungay. The exception was Leiston, whose population increased from 823 in 1801 to 3,259 in 1901, due to the presence of Garrett's engineering works, which dominated the town.

Most of the small market towns did not have sufficient industry to offer employment to the rural worker, while the county towns of Ipswich and Bury St Edmunds were rapidly expanding. The population of Ipswich increased from approximately 11,000 in 1801 to 67,000 in 1901. The opportunity to live and work in Ipswich, earning a good regular wage making agricultural equipment or doing general factory work, would be a strong incentive for a family man to escape the low pay of the farm worker.

In 1874, many farm workers joined the National Agricultural Labourers Union and withdrew their labour over the wage dispute, although they eventually returned for the harvest. Several emigrated to Canada at this time. By then the large grain producers of the American mid west had rail access to the ports, which precipitated greater falls in price. The first shipment of frozen lamb from Australia arrived in 1880.

Our local harvest was, as ever, dependent on the weather, with several very wet years, and others with drought. The 1889 harvest was very poor, with one farmer sending the crop from 16 acres of barley to market on one wagon. Five years later,

the prices were the lowest in living memory, with wheat between 13 and 20 shillings per quarter (1 quarter = 2 coombs). A farm in Worlingworth was put up for auction, but the highest bid was for £9 per acre, and it was withdrawn.

The Royal Commission on Agriculture in 1895 referred to a frightening scene in the countryside, with much arable land turned to grass, and many farmers in the south living from hand to mouth. Henry Rider Haggard travelled throughout the country in 1901 to determine the effects of the agricultural depression. He found that Suffolk

RIGHT: Few small towns could offer factory employment to the rural worker. Leiston was exceptional, with the Garrett engineering works dominating the town. This photo of the boiler shop reeks of heavy industry, with boiler/fire boxes for steam engines, c.1910.

landowners were 'practically ruined' if they had no other source of income, and tenants could only just make a living. Britain's agricultural contribution to the country's economy had fallen from 20% in the 1850s to only 6% in the 1890s. Against this backdrop, it can be seen that for Framlingham, like other small market towns, the core of its economy had been depressed for many years.

Conversely, the economy of the country as a whole was strong and prosperous in 1900. Britain spearheaded the industrial revolution and in the mid-nineteenth century, with only 2% of the world's population, was able to manufacture 40% of the world's goods. By the turn of the century, other countries such as the United States and Germany were catching up. Therefore, although Britain's output had continued to increase, its share of the world market was reducing.

It is difficult to comment on the profitability of local businesses due to the lack of surviving evidence. Most had been in existence for many years and provided necessary services irrespective of the economic climate. There were few non-essential activities, and even the photographer only offered this as a side line to his main business of draper.

Most of the trades were kept busy by repair work. In 1906, for example, the annual turnover of G. & A. Bridges, blacksmiths, was approximately £630, of which 78% was generated from work in the forge, while the remainder was from sales, at a time when they were agents for several well known manufacturers of agricultural equipment. A more revealing fact is that a profit of 17% was made on the turnover. The records also show that all the housekeeping costs were included in the business account, which was usual at a time before all such matters were kept separate. Trade with the blacksmith was essential to keep the horses shod, and to provide a minimum level of maintenance on the farm.

When Frank Baldry started his building firm in 1906, he had £250 cash in the bank, and at the end of the year had made nearly 20% profit on his turnover of £282. However, in the next few years, although the turnover increased annually, the average profit was about 2%.

National data indicate that the average wage of a skilled worker at this time was around £2 per week, with an unskilled labourer at £1 per week. Very long hours would be required to earn that and there would be regional variations. The Suffolk farm worker earned even less.

James Breese's meticulous records show that his highest paid workers, the horsemen, received 14 shillings for a six day week in 1900. The farm steward earned a shilling more, while others earned less. There were normally about ten men

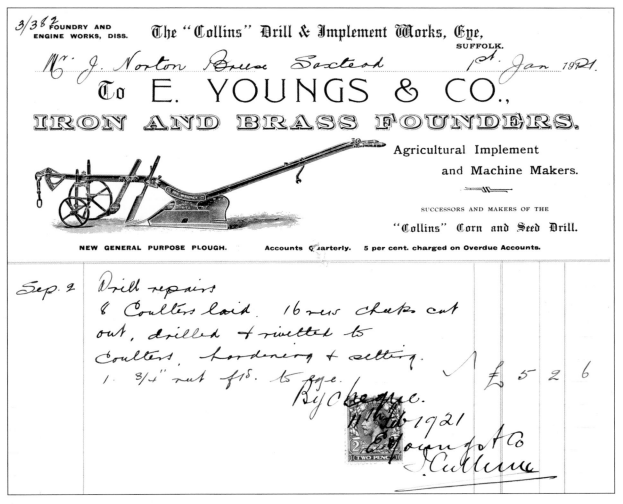

3/38²

FOUNDRY AND
ENGINE WORKS, DISS.

The "Collins" Drill & Implement Works, Eye,
SUFFOLK.

Mr. J. Norton Brese Soxted   1st Jan 1921.

To E. YOUNGS & CO.,

IRON AND BRASS FOUNDERS.

Agricultural Implement
and Machine Makers.

SUCCESSORS AND MAKERS OF THE

"Collins" Corn and Seed Drill.

NEW GENERAL PURPOSE PLOUGH.   Accounts Quarterly.   5 per cent. charged on Overdue Accounts.

Sep. 2   Drill repairs
8 Coulters laid. 16 new chaks cut
out, drilled + rivetted to
coulters, hardening + setting.
1. 3/4" nut fitd. to eye.   √ £ 5 2 6
By Cheque.
11 Nov 1921
E Youngs & Co
J. Cullum

Suffolk was prominent in the manufacture of agricultural machinery, with Ransome and Garrett exporting worldwide. Smaller firms such as E. Youngs and Co. also made an important contribution. This company had an established foundry in Diss where they manufactured a range of agricultural implements, including portable and stationary engines. They acquired William Clowes' drill works in Eye, and this account shows their new Waveney plough.

employed, but this fell to six at times in the winter, and even for them a full week was not guaranteed.

If the farm labourer had opted to move to Ipswich and work for Ransomes in the new century, he would have earned a more regular wage of about 18 shillings a week. At the same period (*c.* 1902), the skilled men in the Ipswich works could earn substantially more:

Engine painter	24*s*
Wheelmaker	26*s*
Boiler maker	34*s*
Ploughman	40*s*
Foreman engine painter	40*s*

Charles Garrard, a local businessman in Framlingham, would have been much better off. In addition to the income from his thriving business, he also received a salary of £100 a year as manager of the gas works.

There is little doubt that living conditions were generally better in rural areas, and less insanitary than in the large towns and cities, where there was often gross overcrowding. Also, there were no large factories with hazardous working conditions. However, the general labourer with a large family would be on poor wages, and any seasonal food from his garden or game that came his way would be important in the weekly struggle to make ends meet. If he did not spend his wages wisely, the family would suffer even more.

It is interesting to attempt a comparison with prices then and now. This has been based on a number of basic purchases such as tea, sugar, tobacco, cheese, soap and sausages from bills of the 1900 period. The costs of the equivalent quantities purchased in Framlingham in 2005 have also been obtained.

Sample of Household Purchases		
1900	2005	Increase Factor
£0 14*s* 9*d*	£24	32.5

The increase varies depending on the mix of goods considered, but also needs to be compared with the change in wages over this time, and two examples have been chosen. The top 1900 pay rates for local agricultural workers are shown at one end of the wage scale, with general guidance for bank managers at the other end.

The 2005 agricultural rate is based on a 39 hour week for a Grade II appointment. The bank manager is based on typical rates for a small branch, excluding bonuses etc. In each case, basic tax and National Insurance have been deducted, to determine a net weekly salary.

Net Weekly Income			
	1900	2005	Increase Factor
Agricultural worker	£0 14s 0d	£212	302.9
Bank manager	£5 6s 0d	£299	56.4

Net Wage Ratio between Bank Manager and Agricultural Worker	
1900	2005
7.6:1	1.4:1

The time required to purchase the earlier range of goods can also be determined, based on a six day working week in 1900, and five day week in 2005.

Number of Days' Work to Purchase Goods		
	1900	2005
Agricultural Worker	6.3	0.6
Bank Manager	0.8	0.4

Such comparisons are fraught with many variables, and can only provide a broad indication of the changes. For example, the pay of some solicitors and doctors in 1900 could be quite low, when starting up in a town where there were established practices.

In 2005, the bank manager's pay depends on the size of the branch and its profitability. Therefore a quite different set of figures would be derived for the manager of a much larger bank, a doctor or established solicitor.

Returning to general commercial life, the building trade was not buoyant at this time, and mainly involved in repairs. Lambert's Almanac for 1897 noted that the town had been quite at a standstill with regard to building operations. In 1902, it was recorded as a noteworthy event that two semi-detached villas had been built in College Road.

There is little evidence of non farming people going out of business due to the economic climate in agriculture, as they were adept at balancing the budget, and with everyone in the same boat, extended credit was the norm. An exception was Mr Roe's bacon factory which opened in 1898 with much publicity, but was in liquidation by 1900.

James Maulden had seen that the future of milling lay in the new roller mill, and invested in the process. The rewards of that investment allowed him to buy Lambert's printing business, and also go into farming.

The businesses within the town catered not only for the residents, some of whom were of independent means, but also provided services to a much wider rural population. The census data for 1901 enable the employment category of the working population to be determined, and this is shown in Appendix 3. For the first time, farm workers are not simply shown as 'ag labs', but allows their more specific title such as the horseman and stockman. The census information related to where people were on the census night, which was a Sunday.

Cranfield's massive new roller mill complex opened in 1884 at Ipswich docks. The rapid advance of the roller mill process heralded the decline of stone ground flour from the traditional windmill, in both town and country.

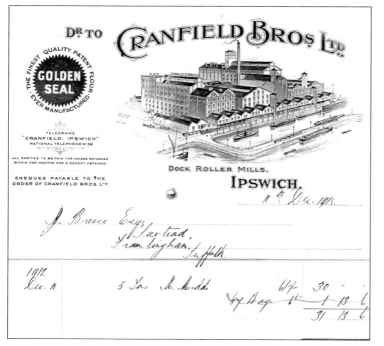

Therefore, anyone who worked in the town but lived outside the parish, or was away on the census day, would be recorded elsewhere.

The practical aspects of transport had a significant effect on the cost of materials and the time taken for delivery. Road conditions prior to the twentieth century were very poor, and the traditions of self sufficiency were paramount, as they always had been. Services or products that could not be locally supplied would have to be brought in. The main method of transporting goods over a long distance in the early nineteenth century was by sea from the nearest ports, which were Ipswich, Slaughden and Woodbridge.

Wagons, pulled by up to six horses, were used for the overland route to London. Passengers could be taken, but this was not for the faint hearted. In the 1820s, Samuel Noller's wagon would leave Framlingham on Thursday night and travel non stop, reaching London on Saturday morning. You would have to question if your journey in company with dead meat for the markets was really necessary. It was not until about 1839 that a faster coach system was put in place from Framlingham. Prior to that, it was necessary to reach Wickham Market to connect with the Yarmouth to London coach.

The advent of the railway was to have a great effect on the country's infrastructure, providing

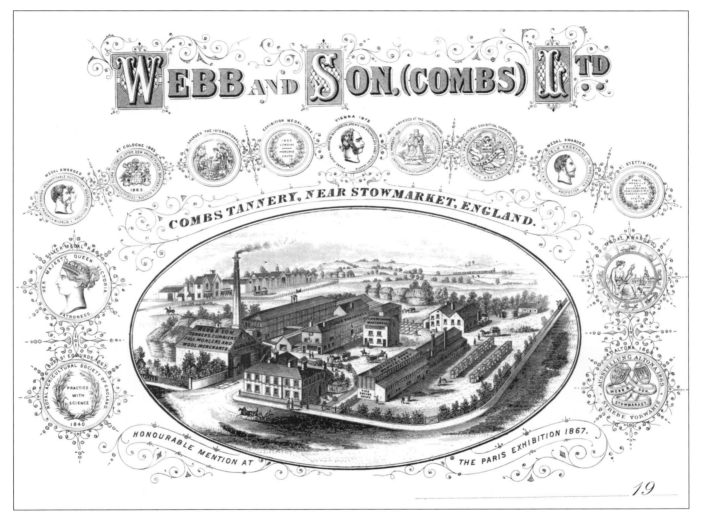

Most towns had a tannery as it was essential to process the animal skins quickly, particularly in hot weather. The origins of the Combs tannery date back to 1710, but it was successive generations of the Webb and Portway families that built up the business, which employed nearly 300 people by the 1880s

faster movement for both goods and people. It also swiftly killed off the established coach trade. Initially, the railway carriages were fully open to the elements and without seats, so the discomfort factor was still high. It was not long though, before you could travel by train in reasonable comfort, arrive in London by mid-morning, have plenty of time for business and be back in Framlingham for the evening. Mr Noller's passengers could not have conceived such a possibility.

The arrival of the railway brought about the greatest change to commercial life in small towns. Although the horse was still essential for the local movement of goods, more distant places could be accessed more quickly and cheaply by rail. The station at Framlingham provided that important link for just over a hundred years, with this photograph being taken in the final period of passenger traffic around 1950.

The opening of the branch line to Framlingham in 1859 marked a change in the life of the town. Not only could people travel greater distances in a day, but goods could be delivered faster and cheaper than before. This had clear benefits in terms of coal supplies, transport of corn etc., but the daily lives of most people would stay largely unchanged, with the population remaining fairly static. The area around the station developed into an industrial site, with granaries and storage for the materials which were transported.

Local transport had not changed though, so movements to and from the station were mainly by horse drawn wagons. There had always been several firms able to supply the skills associated with the carrier and carter, such as wheelwright,

carriage builder, harness maker and blacksmith. Steam traction was not that common for haulage in small towns, although Herbert Manby the corn merchant did buy a Garrett wagon in 1912.

It was not until the twentieth century that the motor vehicle would slowly but surely change our lives. Although motorised vehicles could use public roads at a maximum speed of 12 mph from 1896, it would be a long time before they became a common sight. The First World War gave some people the opportunity to drive vehicles, and following the Armistice large numbers of army lorries became surplus to requirements. These formed a useful basis for a delivery service for the entrepreneur of the day.

The business heart of Framlingham was centred on the Market Hill and surrounding area. The trade evolved from a craft base where goods would be sold from the workshop, through to the development of dedicated shops. The early directories up to around 1850 list 'Shopkeepers' as a category in their own right. This pattern is noticeable in the development of Double Street, but the shops are now gone, and trade crafts have moved further away.

The introduction of the telephone in Framlingham from 1908 can be traced to the larger businesses. Carley's, the established grocers on the Market Hill, was No. 3. This must have been an optimistic move as the likelihood of someone calling would have been slim at the time.

The manner of trading was quite different compared with today, as the economy was closely related to the fortunes of agriculture, which we know were severely depressed from the late 1870s. Bills were rendered quarterly, or over even longer periods, but often not paid until after harvest time. It was common to part pay with goods in kind. For example, Arthur Pendle, the horse slaughterer, might provide grease to offset the amount he would have to pay for dead animals. Grease was essential for axle lubrication on the many farm wagons. The concept of cash flow was well known to local shopkeepers. Even a professional person such as Charles Nesling, the vet, was subject to late payment by his clients, and he was thankful to have Ministry work which paid more regularly.

The greatest changes to have occurred in the twentieth century are due to horse based trades dying out, and being replaced by equivalent services with the motor vehicle. In common with most areas, service industries now predominate, with less actually being manufactured. The self sufficiency of those earlier times has gone. Our present attempts at recycling look rather pathetic against life in Victorian times, when everything was used and eventually recycled, with no wasteful non degradable packaging. Arthur Pendle was a great example of a recycler.

John Self took over Charles Cone's boot shop in 1916. This 2006 photograph shows little change in the external appearance since then.

Arthur George Potter set up as a cooper (barrel maker), basket maker and osier merchant (dealing in the willow shoots for basket manufacture). A skep was a large basket suitable for carrying logs. Potter's reputation is, however, based on his agency for Ford motor cars, established in 1913.

Fortunately, many of the old premises remain, and are readily identified from early photos. Externally, John Self's shoe shop in Albert Place is virtually unchanged, and continues to provide a traditional personal service in the same line of business.

Some companies had a wide range of services that extended beyond the main category, and would also change with time. A. G. Potter is a good example, where his earlier trade of osier merchant and basketmaker developed into bicycles and then on to motor cars and tractors.

People now have more spare time, money and personal transport. There have been extensive housing developments in recent years, and Framlingham has been listed in one survey as the top place to live in the UK. The commercial life of the town will continue to change and adapt to new demands, as it has done in the past. It is worth reflecting on the 100 year period between 1830 and 1930, which spans the business lives of George Brooke Keer, James Maulden and Edwin Clarke. In their time, they were the largest employers in the town, but their names are mostly unknown now. Evolution is a constant process.

Agriculture

Framlingham had long been a centre for agricultural activities in the region when a Farmers Club was formed in 1879. Regular monthly meetings followed, along with the annual show in the castle yard, consisting mainly of poultry, root crops, corn, butter etc. The fortune of the club followed that of agriculture in general, with the poor prices in the early 1890s causing many farmers to quit their tenancies.

The 1901 census shows that there were 25 farms within the parish of Framlingham, providing employment for nearly 22% of the workforce. There were, on average, eight men working on each farm, from the farmer to the general labourer. The horseman always occupied a position of respect on the farm, with the knowledge of his craft and the mysterious customs associated with it.

By the beginning of the twentieth century, many aspects of farming life had changed due to mechanisation and labour shortage. Although the basic ploughing concept remained the same with horses, drilling of the seed was performed by more efficient machinery which had been developed from 1800 by Smyth of Peasenhall, and also Garrett of Leiston. At harvest time the scythe

RIGHT: *Seed drills were made at Smyth's Peasenhall works for over 160 years, but production ceased in the 1960s. This was mainly due to changing technology on the farm, but also because the drills were so well made: one farmer was still using the same drill that had been bought secondhand by his great-grandfather!*

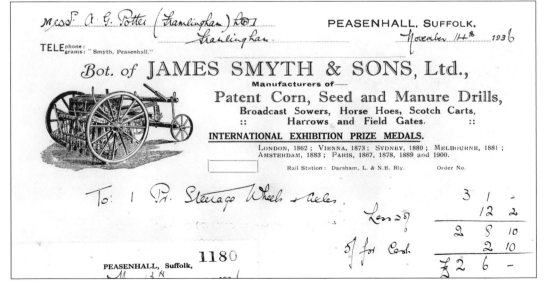

Threshing with a steam powered drum had long been the normal practice by the turn of the century. This 1903, 6hp compound Marshall engine with Clayton and Shuttleworth drum and elevator belonged to John and Arthur Barrell of Coddenham. Such equipment was expensive and many farmers would hire a contractor for the work

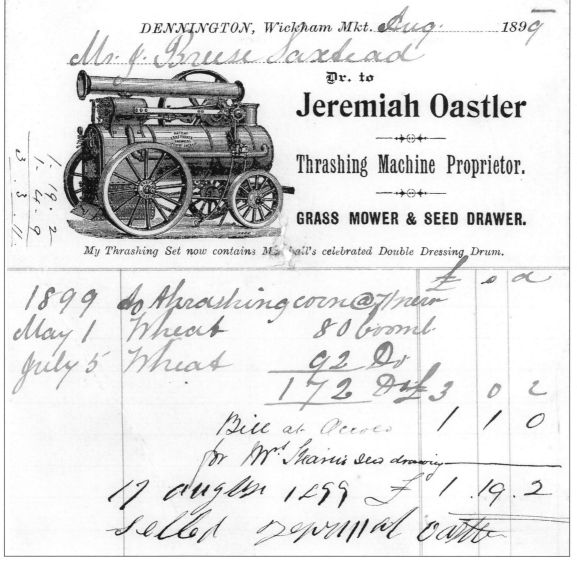

DENNINGTON, Wickham Mkt. *Aug.* 1899

Mr. J. Breese Saxtead

Dr. to
Jeremiah Oastler

---◆◆◆---

Thrashing Machine Proprietor.

---◆◆◆---

GRASS MOWER & SEED DRAWER.

My Thrashing Set now contains Marshall's celebrated Double Dressing Drum.

		£	s	d
1899 May 1	To Thrashing corn @ 7/ new Wheat 80 comb			
July 5	Wheat 92 Do			
	172 Do 3	3	0	2
	Bill at Occes	1	1	0
	for Wm Starns see drawing			
	17 August 1899 £ 1	1	19	2
	Setled Jeremiah Oastler			

Jeremiah Oastler of Dennington was a threshing contractor. His bill shows a portable engine by E. R. & F. Turner of Ipswich, and reference to a Marshall double dressing drum.

was still in use, but a major change had seen the introduction of the sail reaper, followed by the reaper binder in the 1880s. The binder, as its name suggests, could tie the sheaves with twine, but they still had to be collected by hand and gathered into shocks. The flail had long been replaced by the threshing machine, which was operated by steam power, usually belonging to a contractor. Within the barn, a small oil engine might be used to power various machines. There was inevitably a balance to be made between the cost of any new machinery and the reduction in time and labour that it would effect. Despite these advances, the working life of a farm employee remained long and very hard.

Although there was some steam power for ploughing and cultivation, the cart horse was still very much the power on the land and the most practical and economic way for the farmer to operate. There were many cross bred cart horses, but in Suffolk the Punch was the most numerous pure breed with a history going back at least 700 years.

The services of a stallion for breeding were advertised in the newspaper and by handing out 'stallion cards' at local markets and pubs. These cards stated the locations that would be visited in the district, along with details of the fee and the horse's pedigree. The groom would leave the farm on Monday with his stallion and walk the district until their return on Saturday night. He would stay at a farm or pub, and during the day

---

GOLD MEDAL STUD.

1899.

DIMPLE DICK, (2497.)

FOALED, 1894.

THE PROPERTY OF ALFRED J. SMITH, RENDLESHAM,

AT 40/- EACH MARE AND 2/6 THE GROOM.

DIMPLE DICK (2497), has been shown 4 times and won 4 Honours—at the Woodbridge, County, Royal, and Suffolk Shows.

DIMPLE DICK is a dark Chestnut, stands on short legs, with plenty of bone, and an excellent mover, in fact a Farmer's horse all over.

Sire, Queen's Diadem (1721).

Dam, Dimple Darling (2892). Sold to the Earl of Derby.

DIMPLE DICK WILL TRAVEL THE FOLLOWING ROUND IF NOTHING PREVENTS.

Monday —Wickham-Market, Parham, Glemham, Badingham.
Tuesday.—Badingham, Framlingham, Worlingworth.
Wednesday.—Worlingworth, Debenham, Mickfield.
Thursday.—Stonham, Stowmarket, Needham.
Friday.—Coddenham, Ashbocking, Otley.
Saturday.—Clopton, Burgh, Dallinghoo to Eyke.

The money to be paid the first week in June to J. MARKHAM, *the Groom, who is accountable.*

Mares barren last year from any of the Gold Medal Stud Horses, Half-Price.

LODER, PRINTER, WOODBRIDGE.

1899 stallion card for Dimple Dick. The distance travelled in a week by the stallion and his groom could be considerable. In this case it was at least 70 miles, probably more, and was travelled every week between April and June until the mares were known to be in foal.

the stallion would be taken to the mares in the immediate vicinity or they were brought to to him to be covered as previously arranged.

The route might be over 100 miles and this was known as 'travelling a district'. A stallion would cover on average 8–12 mares in a day, with a typical fee of £2 for each mare, along with 2*s* 6*d* being paid to the groom. The same route would be trav-

elled every week between April and June, until the mares were known to be in foal.

Stallions of the Framlingham Heavy Horse Society outside the Crown Hotel in 1938. From the left, Boxted King Hal of W. C. Saunders, Captain John of W. Kindred, and Furneval Facet of A. J. Turner. Local Society members would inspect the stallions and their pedigree before agreeing a fee with the groom for covering their mares.

The blacksmith or ironmonger would often be an agent for various agricultural implement manufacturers. It was necessary to keep spares in stock, and William Barker's Market Hill business (subsequently bought by Charles Garrard in 1897) supplied plough parts such as skimmers, breasts, slides and shares. The famous self-sharpening chilled cast iron plough shares, patented by Robert Ransome in 1803, cost nine shillings per dozen in 1893, while parts for the Woods ploughs made in Stowmarket were also held. Whether the farmer opted to have equipment repaired or replaced, it would usually be the blacksmith who was in a position to help him. Ploughing matches were a regular feature of the Farmers Club, and in 1896 thirty pairs of horses and ploughs assembled on the Market Hill prior to the contest. E. G. Warren, the first headmaster of the new Sir Robert Hitcham's school, became secretary in 1901, which provided

George and Albert Bridges were agents for several agricultural equipment manufacturers. They provided an important service to farmers, particularly in relation to the repair of such equipment, as it would be expected to last for a very long time.

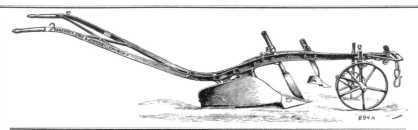

a new lease of life although fortunes continued to fluctuate.

The Suffolk Agricultural Show was held in Framlingham in 1882, and this was a formative event in the founding of the Framlingham Association for the Exhibition of Livestock in 1884, with Charles Austin of Brandeston as chairman and several well known farmers and landowners as patrons. The first Show that year was held on the Castle Meadow. Livestock exhibited included Suffolk horses, cattle, sheep and pigs. In 1885, seventy-two Suffolk foals were shown, and to this day the Show is held in the same location and still graced by the famous Suffolk breed. The name was changed to the Framlingham Livestock Association in 1905.

The Farmers Club was also the catalyst for the formation under the Friendly Societies Act in 1903 of a very successful organisation, originally called the Framlingham and District Agricultural Co-operative Society Ltd. In the first year there were 83 applications for membership, six of

these being clergymen. Premises were initially in Well Close Square, but more space was urgently needed, and Mason's timber yard in Station Road was purchased for £800 in 1904. The company traded in various commodities such as linseed, cotton cake, coal, implements, manures, seeds,

RIGHT: *Prentice Brothers of Stowmarket employed around 40 people in the 1870's, manufacturing fertilisers. The firm was amalgamated in 1929, to become Fison, Packard and Prentice Ltd. The reverse of the account provides the percentages of nitrogen, ammonia and phosphate in the product purchased, along with detailed methods for taking samples in case of dispute.*

corrugated iron, wire netting, and binder twine as well as eggs.

A granary was erected on the site, and experiments were carried out on methods of preserving eggs. Members were also able to hire a cider press. The business grew rapidly, with horse drawn collection vans and a further depot at Stradbroke. It was claimed to be the most successful egg collection society in England, and by 1912 was handling nearly five million eggs annually. A joint venture was established with the Eastern Counties Farmers' Co-operative Association Ltd in Ipswich, although this did not always run smoothly due to overlapping interests.

In 1917 it was agreed that the egg business of that company would be exchanged for the general trade of the Framlingham Society. The company was renamed the Framlingham and Eastern Counties Co-operative Egg and Poultry Society Ltd., with its head office in Ipswich. The business prospered during the First World War, and Mr Warren was asked to leave his school activities to become full time Secretary. The company was compelled to employ women in the office and depot, as so many men were away fighting. The railway was essential for the large scale movement of eggs, and the GER costs in 1912 were £861. A new model packing station was opened in Badingham Road in 1949, with over 62 million eggs being collected in 1952.

Framlingham and District Agricultural Co-operative Society Ltd. was formed in 1903, and moved to these premises in Station Road a year later. By 1907, it was the largest egg collection society in England with further depots in Debenham, Ipswich and Stradbroke.

The Auctioneer

Commercial life revolves around buying and selling, be it houses, estates, livestock, deadstock or any other commodity. Framlingham had the benefit of its own sale yard in Bridge Street, where Robert Bond of Ipswich was holding auctions in the 1870s.

In 1900, Bond's sale yards were at Ipswich, Eye and Woodbridge, where the commission charged was as follows:

horses	1s 0d in the pound
pigs	6d in the pound
lambs and hoggets	8s 6d per score
fat lambs and tups	1s 0d in the pound
cows and heifers	2s 6d, value <£9
	5s 0d, value >£9

However, it was Alfred Preston from Worlingworth who was to establish himself firmly in Framlingham,

Receipt for pigs bought at the sale yard in 1903, including commission and insurance.

several long established firms in the county. They were all kept busy in the late Victorian period by farm and land sales, due to the perilous state of farming at that time. In one of Preston's advertisements from 1905 there were 20 different farms to be auctioned over a two month period.

Farm and general property sales were often conducted at the Crown Hotel, where, for example, he sold the Earl Soham post mill with outbuildings and around 25 acres for £545 in 1899. On the fall of the hammer, it was necessary for the buyer to hand over 10% of the purchase price, with the remainder being due within about three months.

When the tenancy of a farm changed there would often be an auction, which was always a popular social occasion. Preston was well known throughout the county for his lively auctions. The arrival of this tall, well dressed and domineering figure was heralded by the ringing of a bell. If the sales were slow, it was not unknown for him to offer to lend the bidder some money. An example of his sales pitch is illustrated by one lot which was a sack lifter, when he proclaimed that he would never work on a farm that did not have one.

This was a financially rewarding business due to the extent of his work. Typical fees for farm valuations might vary between about 3% on £100 value, down to 1.3% on £1,000 value. The £13 gained for

holding regular Saturday auctions at the sale yard. A typical sale advertised in 1899 had 230 pigs, 11 cows, two horses, 250 sheets of corrugated iron, along with hoes, harrows, corn sacks, hen coops and a tumbrel. By 1900, he was holding additional sales on a Monday, and would eventually take premises on the Market Hill next to Coleman the bootmaker, trading as auctioneer, valuer, house and estate agent. The traditional way of selling goods and houses was by auction and there were

the latter would be equivalent to about 18 weeks' wages for a horseman on the farm. By 1910, like other professionals, Preston saw the need to have a motor car and bought a very fine Siddeley Deasy, costing around £900, in which he was chauffeur driven to the auctions, markets and his Ipswich office. There was local competition in Charles Read, who had a long established office in College Road, and now offered the joint skills of accountant and auctioneer.

During the First World War, Preston conducted Red Cross auctions at the Sale Yard, where contributions were provided by local businessmen and dignitaries such as the Marquis of Graham and the Duchess of Hamilton. Their home, Easton Park, was in use as a Red Cross hospital, and several of the wounded were brought along to view the sale.

In 1918, there was a significant sale of the Suffolk Horse Stud at Sudbourne Hall. This realised the

Alfred Preston holding a Red Cross Sale in 1917. He is standing in the front of his Siddeley Deasy car, with Sir Robert Hitcham's almshouses in the background.

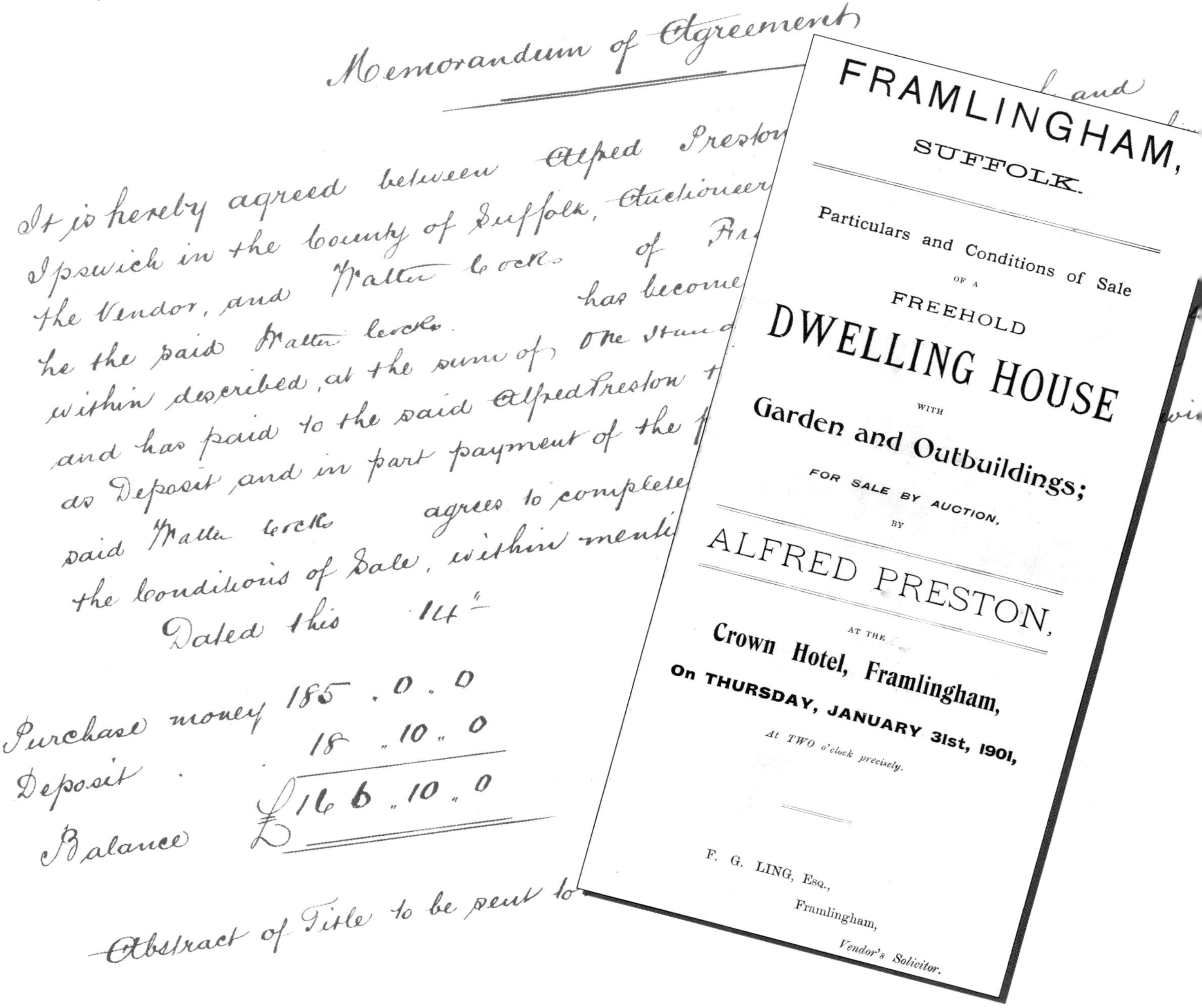

Memorandum of Agreement

It is hereby agreed between Alfred Preston
Ipswich in the County of Suffolk, Auctioneer
the Vendor, and Walter Cocks of Fra
he the said Walter Cocks has become
within described, at the sum of One Hun
and has paid to the said Alfred Preston t
as Deposit and in part payment of the p
said Walter Cocks agrees to complete
the Conditions of Sale, within menti
Dated this 14th

Purchase money 185 . 0 . 0
Deposit 18 . 10 . 0
Balance £166 . 10 . 0

Abstract of Title to be sent to

FRAMLINGHAM,
SUFFOLK.

Particulars and Conditions of Sale
OF A
FREEHOLD
DWELLING HOUSE
WITH
Garden and Outbuildings;
FOR SALE BY AUCTION,
BY
ALFRED PRESTON,
AT THE
Crown Hotel, Framlingham,
On THURSDAY, JANUARY 31st, 1901,
At TWO o'clock precisely.

F. G. LING, Esq.,
Framlingham,
Vendor's Solicitor.

ABOVE: *Woodward's sale yard in Station Road, Stowmarket. George Woodward had been an articled pupil with Garrod and Turner of Ipswich before starting his own business around 1900. Stowmarket would later become one of the largest pig markets in the country.*

substantial sum of £33,180, of which Preston received 5%, to cover the financial risk, printing of posting bills and catalogues, advertising in various papers, including the *New York Herald*, helpers at sale, police attendance etc. Along with auctions of three associated farms on the estate, Preston's overall commission was in excess of £2,500.

LEFT: *1901 sale document. Walter Cocks bought this property in Fore Street for £185. A 10% deposit had to be paid at the auction. The sale particulars were printed in Framlingham by Henry Damant.*

When Alfred Preston retired, Moore Garrard and Son took over, and by 1929 were owners of the sale yard, which was then in use on alternate Fridays. Increased mobility of stock by lorry to larger markets meant that business declined. A report in 1937 referred to it as 'Framlingham's forgotten market', with 12 'disinterested' people, a few hens, some iron tanks and packing cases. The sale yard inevitably closed for ever in that year.

The Baker

Bread is the staple part of our diet, and in any town there would be several bakers, along with millers to provide them with the basic ingredients. The life of a baker was arduous, involving a very early start at around 3 a.m., moving the heavy sacks of flour and enduring the heat of the ovens.

Bread is made from dough whose main ingredients are flour, salt, yeast and water, which are kneaded and then put in metal trays, covered and allowed to rise. Each baker would have his own variations and special ingredients which, combined with different grades of flour, yielded a wide range of loaves. It is generally considered that bread made from the traditional darker stone ground flour has more flavour and goodness than the whiter roller mill flour. Wheat flour is the mainstay for bread production, because of its superior colour, flavour, yield and ability to achieve a loaf that rises well. In earlier times, barley and rye had also been used for bread.

Interior of Mayhew's bakery in Ipswich Street, Stowmarket. William Mayhew, centre, is holding the peel which was used to take the loaves in and out of the ovens, whose doors are visible in the background.

The baker required a regular supply of flour, which would be provided by the local miller. The 1901 census data show that there were eight men employed as millers' carters. These men would need to be strong, as the sack of flour was very heavy, weighing 20 stones.

The oven was heated by burning faggots of dried blackthorn or whitethorn until the temperature reached between about 420 and 480° Fahrenheit.

In 1912, Fred Holmes took over the Market Hill premises where Middleton the confectioner had traded for many years. He proudly stands by his sprung tradesman's cart.

This might be determined by rubbing a piece of wood against the oven or throwing some flour on it and watching for sparks. The loaves were then put into the oven using a long handled device with a flat end called a peel, and left to bake for about an hour. The process was repeated daily in order to satisfy the needs of customers near and far. Home baking had been the norm in rural areas, but with improvements in transport there was greater reliance on the baker, with Simpson delivering to villages as far away as Sibton, nine miles distant.

A bakery required substantial ovens, so it is not surprising that the trade carried on in the same building through several changes of ownership. Spencer Leek acquired property in Well Close Square, where he and his wife Ann had a confectionery business. These were the same premises that William Simpson took over in 1886, as confectioner and baker, having been house steward at Framlingham College for many years. This was a period when the College was in financial difficulty, with several staff having pay cuts, and William being given notice to leave. He became proficient in his new trade, and received a Hovis diploma of merit in 1905. William and his wife had thirteen children, and it was his sixth son, George,

Army Service Corps personnel in Holmes' bakery, 1915. Fred is standing in the centre, with his men Cecil (left) and Frederick Sherman either side. The photo was taken by C. F. Dowsing, a local photographer.

William Simpson started his bakery business in Well Close Square in 1886. At the time of this receipt, his diploma of merit had only recently been received.

Albert Place was prone to regular flooding. Deliveries by horse and cart to Arthur Bonney's bakery were hardly affected, but handling the 20-stone sacks of flour under these conditions would have been more difficult than usual.

who took over the business on his father's retirement. He died in 1928 after a heavy fall on the back step of the bakery. It then passed to Bob Simpson, a grandson of William.

Another long established name connected with baking was Arthur Bonney. He started as a baker, confectioner and flour dealer in 1881, from his premises on the corner of Fore Street and Station Road. Along with Simpson, these two names were synonymous with the craft of baking in Framlingham for many years.

Edwin Middleton's confectionery shop on the Market Hill could provide a range of christening, wedding and birthday cakes as well as more exotic fare such as Assam tea, oranges, figs, coker (*sic*) nuts, Bosnian plums, German yeast and Quinine wine. Robert Middleton was running the shop from at least 1877, being taken over by Edwin in 1885, until about 1910. He described himself as a pastry cook, but was also able to cater for wedding breakfasts, ball suppers and parties.

There is now only one baker in Framlingham. Although no longer troubled by the need to find faggots for the fire, an early rise is still required.

Bought of E. MIDDLETON,
WHOLESALE AND RETAIL
Pastry-Cook, Confectioner, Fruiterer, Etc.

DEALER IN BRITISH AND FOREIGN WINES

Bride Cakes	Lemonade	Assam Tea
Sponge Cakes	Gingerade	Pickles
Tea Cakes [Biscuits	Soda Water	Preserved Fruits
Huntley & Palmer's	Quinine Wine	German Yeast

Sponge Shape   1 6
   ,,   Cakes   6
Sweets   2
Almonds   11

Banking

The growth of business, and goods arriving from remote places via the railways, meant that efficient systems for the payments and receipts of services were required. It was often the case that prominent tradesmen became involved with financial businesses. George Edwards was a wealthy grocer in the 1820s and became treasurer and manager of the Framlingham Savings Bank. On his death in 1877 it was carried on by S. G. Carley, also a grocer.

The early banks were represented by local agents, with the Edwards brothers on the Market Hill looking after the interests of Gurney and Co. of Norwich, whose presence was established in the town by 1808. This company had a bewildering number of name changes through the century.

They would not have been pleased when Harvey and Hudson (Crown Bank), opened up in Church Street, with Mr Bloom as their agent, there being strong competition between them. In 1855, Harvey and Hudson bought the site of the present Barclays Bank, and constructed new premises, although their tenure was relatively short lived. The senior partner of the company, Sir Robert Harvey, had speculated on the Stock Exchange, but the Franco Prussian War created a major drop in prices which ruined him. He shot himself on 15th July 1870, and on the next day the bank closed.

The property and goodwill of the company were bought by the Gurney Bank, and in 1873 the new Market Hill premises opened for business. Lambert's Almanac noted that 'the building is both an ornament to the town and a credit to Messrs. Smyth of Aldeburgh, the contractors'. By 1891, the Framlingham branch was under the control of the Halesworth partnership of the group, with Charles Kidall as manager. The partnership name was 'Gurneys Birkbeck Barclays Buxtons and Orde', which was to become part of Barclays Bank and Co. Ltd.

Banks in the smaller towns were usually established in an existing building. Barclays Bank, Needham Market in 1937, had a brick façade on a much older structure. Their telephone number was an unforgettable No 1. The same premises are still used by the bank, although the dormer windows no longer exist.

This Barclays Bank cheque of 1922 still bears reference to the Gurney origins.

Typical bank interior 1907. Note the electric lamps and cheerful disposition of the staff.

The restriction of private banks was their limit of six partners who all had unlimited liability, which affected their ability to help firms that needed to borrow large amounts of capital. So it was, then, that 20 banks amalgamated in 1896 to form Barclay and Company Ltd, with 182 branches.

Many of them had strong Quaker traditions, including Gurneys, which was the largest country bank, having evolved from cloth merchants in Norwich.

The annual salary of a branch manager around 1900 would depend on the size of the bank, along with his years of employment. Typically, it would have been in the range of £250–£300 for an experienced man in a small town. Some women were first employed in banking during the First World War, but it was not until 1958 that the first female manager was appointed by Barclays. Clerks' wages were between £85 and £145, depending on grade, and young apprentices earned £30 per year. The clerks had a £15 pay rise on alternate years. Business hours were between 10 a.m. and 4 p.m., except on Wednesday when they closed at 1 p.m.. Market day and Saturday saw extended opening until 5 p.m..

Correspondence from the bank was mainly hand written, with carbon copies being retained as a record. Clients could be provided with bills of exchange, advances and overdraft facilities. The details of the account were kept in a small white leather bound book, which had a built in pocket for the cheques that were returned to the customer after clearance. The book was kept by the customer, but made up monthly by the bank.

Every six months, charges were added to the account, which at that time were determined solely by the local manager who would know all his customers well. For example, in 1908, Frank Baldry paid half year commissions on his account of 13s 4*d* and 14*s* 6*d*. Money would also be deposited with the bank. The Gas Light Company had £200 on deposit in 1900, on which they received 2% interest each year.

The bank would trade in stocks and shares on behalf of their customers. Insurance was not sold by the bank, but staff were allowed to act as agents for other companies that banked with Barclays, provided they had been approached by that company. The manager would usually be the agent, and also receive the commission.

In 1918, Barclays Head Office instructed that the commissions on Life and Fire policies had to be paid into a separate agency account, and that half of it would be payable to the bank. Even so, such arrangements were a significant boost to salary, and on retirement the employee would be allowed to continue the agency. If it was relinquished, a payment equivalent to two years of average commission would be paid to that person.

It was not until 1919 that Lloyds Bank bought No. 12 Market Hill. Their presence in Framlingham was relatively short lived, as they closed this branch in 1941 as part of an agreement with Barclays in relation to overall business in Suffolk.

Sombre-faced clerks surrounded by ledgers. It would appear from the two shades that electric lighting has recently been installed, but the gas light has been retained.

The Blacksmith

The blacksmith provided many services, not only to the local farmers but to anyone who needed metal to be fashioned or repaired. The range of ironwork in buildings would be made by the blacksmith, much of it still in existence today. One aspect of his trade involved working closely with the wheelwright, to make the iron tyre for the wooden

Jennings and Martin were wheelwrights and smiths, with their forge in Ash Street, Semer. Note the two iron tyres to the left, and set of harrows against the wall. This photograph, with Walter Martin in the centre, is from around 1930.

Tom Card and Hector Moore at Brandeston forge. They have just set the heated tyre over the wheel, and water has been poured on to stop the felloes from burning. Hector is screwing down the nave to prevent the contracting tyre from forcing it upwards. In 1955, Hector was fitting tyres to wheels for Smyth seed drills, witnessing the final period of a very long tradition.

wheels. The earlier wheels were straked, which meant the tyre was made up from a number of curved sections (strakes), which were nailed to the felloe (rim), across the joints. Felloes were called 'fellies' in Suffolk. A special device, called the samson, was used to contract the rim before fitting the strake. The continuous tyre had replaced the strake for new wheels by the late 1800s, and this was formed in a rolling machine to obtain the correct circumference, when the two ends of the hoop were fire welded together. The whole tyre would then be heated in the forge, or an outside fire, and placed over the rim with the hub fixed to a large metal plate in the ground. When evenly hammered into place, water was poured over it, which made the whole wheel contract tightly.

The blacksmith was, in most places, also a farrier or shoeing smith and would serve a four year apprenticeship. He would start work at 6.30 a.m., with a break at 8.00 a.m. for breakfast, usually cold bacon in large slices of bread, washed down with cold tea from a beer bottle. The hearth and anvil were the focal points of his work, with a hand operated bellows to force the fire. Horse shoes were made of wrought iron, and it was common to make them from old shoes or scrap metal, which were fire welded together. Old scrap iron was often taken in part payment of bills.

Hot shoeing of the horse took place in the travus, which is a name derived from trave house, the trave being a frame to hold an unruly horse. The shoe is heated in the furnace, then shaped on the anvil before being pressed against the horse's hoof to ensure a good fit. Holes for the nails were punched

on the anvil prior to fixing the shoe with special horse nails. The protruding ends were twisted off and clenched over, before tidying up the hoof

The temperature needed for welding or bending metal would be judged from its colour when taken from the fire. Blacksmiths such as Joe Bugg of Old Newton had long experience in all aspects of metal craft.

with a rasp file. The typical cost for shoeing a cart horse in 1900 was 2*s* 8*d*. In winter conditions heavy horses had difficulty gaining grip on icy roads, and it was common to use special protruding 'frost nails'. These were either in the form of a nail, or alternatively screwed into a tapped hole in the shoe.

There were many other jobs required of the blacksmith. A common one was the replacement of the worn out tines in a set of harrows. The new tine would be made from stock bar which had been heated cherry red, and cut with a chisel on the anvil. The four sides on one end would be formed to a point, while the other was made cylindrical over a length of about 2 inches. This end would then be put in the hand operated threading machine to produce a coarse thread, on to which a large square nut was placed. Using such methods, a set of harrows could be repaired for ever.

Fruer Bridges' bill of 1894 for various parts of a Ransome plough. The slade was fixed to the underside of the plough body and slid along the bottom of the furrow, and therefore subject to regular replacement.

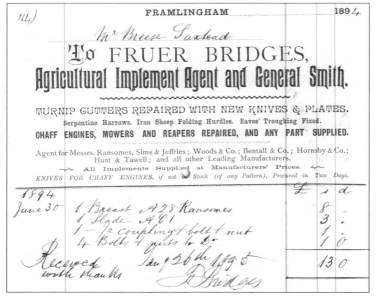

Silvanus Bridges came to Framlingham in about 1724 and set up as a blacksmith in Double Street. His grandson, John, followed the same trade but eventually took separate premises on the corner of Fairfield Road and Fore Street. His grandson, Fruer Bridges, started his working life in the office of William Edwards, the solicitor in Double Street, before taking a similar post in London. On his father's death he returned to the blacksmith business and built it up, eventually taking on agencies for several agricultural implement manufacturers such as Bamford, Bentall, Blackstone, Cornish and Lloyd, Garrett, Ransomes and Sims, Ruston Hornsby and Wolseley Sheep Shearing. By 1881 he was employing three men and two apprentices.

When Fruer died in 1905, the business passed to his two sons, George and Albert. Two years later, an ironmongery shop was built on to the forge in

Fore Street. From the late nineteenth century, the business had expanded considerably, with the shoeing and ironwork being handled by additional staff. In 1920, there were up to seven men employed, with three hearths in the forge on the corner of Fairfield Road. Wages for the skilled men at that time were between £2 and £2 15s 0d for a 51 hour working week.

There was always a number of blacksmiths plying their trade at any one time, as there was such a demand, which continued through World War 2. James Rose also had a long established blacksmith shop in College Road, which passed to W. & C. Girling in 1912. The new owners had an inauspicious start, as their premises were burnt down along with the adjacent thatched cottage in the same year. Gordon Sly recalled that as a young boy in the 1930s he would take his father's horses into the town to be shod. There would sometimes be such a queue of horses waiting outside the Fore Street travus that he would continue on to James Fairhead who was by then running the College Road shop, where his father also had an account. Bad weather conditions would hinder work on the farm, and this was seen as a good time to have the horses shod.

The bill of James Rose shows that four new horse shoes cost 2s 8d in 1911, but only 4d to add frost nails to two shoes. These were necessary in winter to gain extra grip on the icy roads.

FRAMLINGHAM, Dec 31 1916

Mr Jas Brease Farmer Saxted

Dr. to JAMES ROSE,
SHOEING SMITH.

Accounts Rendered Quarterly.

		s	d
Feb 19	new hoop to nave for waggon wheel	2	0
Mar 15	draft eye laide & screwed	"	6
18	4 new shoes	2	8
21	spindle drilled & repaired & new pin	1	0
June 20	one new shoe	"	8
24	one new shoe	"	8
July 5	one shoe removed	"	4
16	handle mended & repaired to rake	"	10
20	chisel put on to walkingstick	"	4
22	2 new shoes & 2 nails	1	7
26	2 new shoes	1	4
Aug 12	2 new shoes	1	4
17	new spindle & screwed to rape machine	3	10
27	4 new shoes	2	8
Sept 30	one new shoe	"	8
Oct 13	drill counter repaired & rivets to plates	"	4
29	draft bolt mended	"	8
Nov 14	4 new shoes	2	8
18	2 shoes steel frost nails	"	4
19	one new shoe	"	8
21	2 new shoes & 2 removed	2	0
		£1	7 1

Settled Jan 6 1911 Jas Rose with Thanks

The blacksmith shop was a great meeting place, with an opportunity to exchange gossip and keep warm by the fire. Girling's blacksmith shop is still recognisable, close to the White Horse Inn. The last blacksmith in the town was Ernie Levett *(pictured on page 13)*, who retired from the Fairfield Road forge in 1964.

Bert Wright shoeing a horse in Fore Street, c.1910, while behind him is George Kerridge, the head blacksmith, both wearing their leather aprons. On the right, with cloth apron, is his son, Alfred Kerridge, who worked for Coleman the shoemaker. The forge was a popular meeting place, although to the detriment of the blacksmith getting on with his job.

The Bootmaker

Comfortable, durable boots and shoes were essential when roads were in poor condition and considerable distances had to be covered on foot. The shoemaker traditionally made shoes, but towards the end of the 1800s, ready made shoes were making substantial inroads to this craft. Special factories in Norwich and Northampton, for example, could manufacture 600 pairs of shoes each day by the 1860s. The introduction of the Singer sewing machine from America, when adapted for leather, along with additional mechanisation, was to transform the industry. By the turn of the century, the local shoemaker was still capable of making shoes, and continued to do so for his wealthier clients, particularly for specialist footwear such as hunting boots. The larger business with shop front premises was now selling ready made shoes, but there was still plenty of work for the cobbler as repairs would always be needed.

Henry Coleman had premises on the Market Hill, and proudly proclaimed that he was 'patronised by the Duke and Duchess of Hamilton and Brandon', who lived at Easton Park. This is another trade which was self sufficient within the town. Leather hides could be purchased from the tannery in Bridge Street, with the thicker parts for the insole and uppers. The shoemaker had a range of formers or 'lasts' which were made of wood, in two parts, to cover a wide range of shoe sizes, and were individual to each customer. He also used an impressive range of tools with names such as clicking knife, last hook, welt pricker, pattern awls, toe beaters, nippers, pincers and fudge wheel. He would sit on his stool, which had its own work surface along with separate open compartments for the various sizes of nails that were required. The foot last held the shoe so that both hands were free to work on it.

The upper parts of the shoe were cut to shape with a long knife and stitched with thread made from hempen fibre twisted together with cobbler's wax. A pig's bristle would be fixed in the end to ease it through the hole. The stitching required consider-

Henry Coleman standing in the doorway of his Market Hill premises. He promoted his trade through the patronage of the local nobility. To the right is Alfred Kerridge, who later set up his own business in Fore Street.

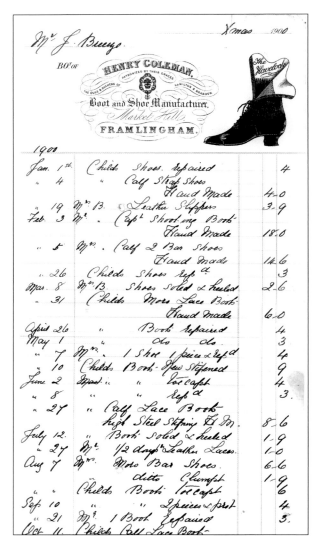

A number of new hand-made boots and shoes are identified in Coleman's 1900 account.

able pressure to be applied, and a special leather glove was used to prevent the thread cutting into the hand. Several layers of leather of varying thickness were soaked, and then beaten with a hammer in order to make up the sole.

The welt is the important strip that joins the upper part of the shoe to the sole, and was often bought from the tanner where it had been specially treated with an oil and wax mix as a waterproofing agent. Finally, the sole and heel were fixed to the insole

BELOW: *In 1901, Charles Cone was 77 years old, and described in the census as a bootmaker, with his son Charles as assistant. This advert is from Lambert's Family Almanac. John Self took over the business in 1916. The premises in Albert Place are still in use as a shoe shop, and externally little changed from Charles Cone's time.*

using wooden pegs, prior to smoothing and cleaning all surfaces. Heel-ball was a mixture of wax and lamp black, applied with a heated iron to ensure that the heel and sole would be watertight.

The shoemaker was a very skilled person and it was easy for him to vary the shoe or boot to suit individual requirements. It was also a trade that lent itself well to the self employed. In the 1901 census for Framlingham, there are 12 self employed boot/shoemakers out of a total of 24 in the trade.

Charles Cone had his boot and shoe shop in Albert Place for many years. On his death in 1916, it was purchased by John Self, who advertised it as a 'boot and shoe warehouse'. The time of the handmade shoe for everyday use was passing.

Henry Coleman could still make a good pair of boots costing around 18 shillings at that time; they would have a long life as they could be repaired many times. The farmworkers all wore boots which had large studs in the sole, and metal heel plates to extend their life. His advertisements of 1900 referred to 'everything in the trade made to order', along with being an agent for various manufacturers, but by 1918, 'hand made' shoes had been mainly replaced by cheaper products from the factory. The shoe repairer still existed in Framlingham well into the second half of the twentieth century. Asher Symonds, who had been apprenticed to Coleman, was still at work in his Riverside (previously called Bridge Street) shop until 1972. Some of the tools associated with his trade are displayed in the museum in the castle. John Self's original shop still provides a good traditional shoe service in the twenty-first century.

RIGHT: *Asher Symonds was apprenticed to Henry Coleman, and was still repairing shoes in his own Riverside shop until his retirement in 1972.*

The occasion of this photograph is unknown. Note the variety of drinking vessels, and the barrels from Cobbold and Co. of Ipswich.

The Brewer and Publican

Beer was a very important part of the everyday diet of men, women and children at a time when the purity of water could not be assured. It was a natural part of working life. The Framlingham fire engine crew would not leave for a fire before ensuring the beer was on board, and it was also provided when a colt was shod by the blacksmith for the first time.

RIGHT: *Tom Page's brewery was located at the rear of the Castle Inn. Photo dated 1949. The wall surrounding the castle pond still existed then.*

The 1830 Beerhouse Act permitted any householder assessed for the poor rate to obtain an Excise Licence to retail beer from his own dwelling, either as an 'on' or 'off' sale, on payment of two guineas. Small-scale brewing was wide-

spread, and a number of beer retailers are noted in the town through the 1870s. In the same period John Chaplin was brewing ale and porter at the Castle Brewery. These premises were built by Benjamin Rackham, and originally were called the Black Swan and Castle. Castle Street was previously called Swan Street. However, it was J. T. (Tom) Page, who built up this business. He married a brewer's daughter, and moved in 1881 to Framlingham, where he took over and subsequently purchased the Castle Brewery. His adverts claimed that the beer was guaranteed brewed from malt and hops only, with no sugar or other substitutes added. The beer was sold in 4½ (pin), 9 (firkin), 18 (kilderkin) or 36 (barrel) gallon casks, from 10*d* per gallon upwards.

This 1902 receipt shows the range of beers available, and was printed by 'Maulden & Sons, steam printers'. Malt and hops were also available from the brewery.

Bill from the final period of brewing. A firkin is nine gallons, and a kilderkin 18 gallons.

Beer is produced by mashing crushed malt with water, always called 'liquor' by the brewer. The barley malt was obtainable from E. G. Clarke's Haynings malting in nearby Castle Street, or from James Maulden in Bridge Street. After the crushing process, the malt (grist) is then transferred to a vessel called the mash tun, containing the liquor, where the starch is converted by enzymes to sugar. The liquid, known as the 'wort', passes to a collecting vessel before being boiled in a large copper, where the hops are introduced. Although Kent is traditionally thought of as the county for hop production, they were also grown in the Stowmarket area in the early nineteenth century. It is the boiling time and process that releases the flavours from the hops, to provide the character of the beer, while also sterilising the wort and preventing further enzyme action. On cooling, it is transferred to a fermenting vessel, where the yeast is added at a controlled temperature to turn the sugar to alcohol, a process lasting four to eight days.

In the larger towns the breweries expanded and bought up pubs to become 'tied houses', i.e. they were tied to selling beer from the owning brewery. By the 1890s, Tom Page was also an agent for Greene's Bury ales, and Truman Hanbury and Buxton's bottled ales. He sold the business in 1904, along with a pub in Saxmundham, to the latter company. From

that time brewing ceased, and Arthur Newson became landlord. All beer then arrived at the station in 18 gallon casks from London. These were taken to the brewery where they were put on a stand and the bottles filled by a gravity fed pipe system. Once

Frederick Rix was landlord of the Station Hotel in the 1920s. Good stabling and a garage were advertised as an inducement to visit the premises.

Mr Fisk at the bar of the Castle Inn, with Frank Newson about to pull a pint, c.1947.

a month, all the empty casks were taken by horse and dray to the station, to be returned to Trumans for refilling. When Arthur Newson retired in 1925, his namesake took over, but they were not related.

In an earlier time, Framlingham was ahead of the county generally when George Brooke Keer built his large malting and brewing operation around the Fore Street/Crown and Anchor Lane corner. Part of that output went to the 21 pubs that he owned in the town and surrounding areas. For a small town, this was a major development, before tied pubs became the norm many years later. Brooke Keer's bankruptcy in 1832 due to non payment of malt taxes had a significant effect on the town, as he was the major employer at the time.

In 1900 there were the following licensed premises in Framlingham:

Castle Inn *Castle Street*
Crown and Anchor *Church Street*
Crown Hotel *Market Hill*
Farrier's Arms *Double Street*
Hare and Hounds *Castle Street*
Queen's Head *Market Hill*
Railway Inn *Station Road*
Station Hotel *Station Road*
White Horse *College Road*

This is a considerable reduction from the 16 inns that existed around 1750. Although beer has not been commercially brewed in the town for over a hundred years, the Castle Inn is still sometimes referred to as 'the brewery'.

The Hare and Hounds and the Queen's Head were bought by the Colchester Brewing Co. Ltd, but eventually sold on, and then owned by E. Lacon and Co. Ltd, the Great Yarmouth brewer. Along with the Farrier's Arms at the lower end of Double Street, these pubs have not survived into the twenty-first century.

The Hare and Hounds, on the corner of Castle Street and Double Street. (For an interior view, see page 185.) In the distance, the black buildings are the Haynings maltings, last operated by E. G. Clarke in the 1930s.

The Builder and Brickmaker

By the late 1800s, the number of builders in the town had fallen considerably compared with the beginning of the century. Even the building of the Albert Memorial College from 1863 did little to further expansion within the town. That contract was awarded to J. W. Lacey of Norwich. Two men were killed during the construction, highlighting the ever present risks.

The name Mallows was synonymous with building for many years, with the founder originally being foreman to John Fruer, a leading tradesman who

Frank Baldry's premises in Station Road, with two of his workmen, Arthur Scotchmer and Walter Leech. Baldry took over Charles Goodwin's business in 1906.

in 1823 built the Congregational Church in Fore Street. Mallows' premises were in Station Road, along with Frank Baldry, who took over Charles Goodwin's business in 1906. There was little house building at the time, but one of Baldry's first contracts was for three new houses in Fore Street, to replace those lost in a disastrous fire. The firm expanded in 1911 by incorporating the plumbing and painting business of John Howlett. Baldry also provided a funeral service, with the typical cost in 1906 varying between £2 and £4. The latter would include a polished oak coffin with calico lining and brass fittings.

Building materials could be purchased from George Mason's depot in Station Road, which

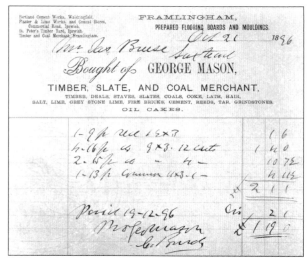

George Mason had a depot in Station Road until 1904 and would be known today as a builders' merchant. They stocked a wide range of goods, but not bricks, which were always locally made.

sold timber, slate, staves, laths, lime and cement. Mason's manufactured cement in their own works at Waldringfield.

The builder would need to be proficient in many areas. Internal surfaces would have a smooth hair

Preparing render for the walls of a cottage.

mortar finish, either applied directly to the brick wall or over horizontal wood laths on a stud wall or ceiling. The mortar was made by mixing lime with water, which was then poured into a circle of sand. Ox hair was traditionally added, and all mixed together. On setting, it provided a very durable finish which resisted cracking on walls and ceilings. He would also take on tasks such as rebuilding chimneys, inserting slate damp proof courses and underpinning, which would all draw on the builder's wealth of experience.

The Victorian builder was not troubled by the mass of services that are necessary today, but it was still a long process to build a house, with only manual labour available. The vertical sliding sash windows,

House nearing completion in Station Road, Framlingham. Note the spaces left in the brickwork for timber scaffolding, yet to be filled.

for example, would be made by a carpenter working for the builder. Each room would have a fireplace, and these could be important for drying out the property on completion. The wet mortar finish applied to the walls and ceilings could take many months to dry out before the house would be ready for occupation.

The main components of any building were the bricks, and these were made in a local works. The large quantity required for the College were made on site, as there was a good source of brick earth at the foot of the hill in front. Thomas Twidell Buckmaster was primarily a corn miller and coal merchant, but he also developed a brickyard in

Station Road, although it had ceased operation by the end of the century.

Peter Smith was from an established family of brickmakers in Badingham. He moved to Framlingham and started the brick and tile works between Kettleburgh Road and Broadwater, which were operated until about 1935 by his son William. Around 1900 they employed at least eight people.

Bricks are made from various types of clay, which are dug from the ground. Special narrow bladed spades were used, and during the winter months a reduced workforce would stockpile the clay, when the action of the rain and frost would break it down. The clay was then crushed and mixed with sand and water in a horse driven pug mill, and the elastic compound cut into blocks. The brick maker would then use a mould which contained a block to form the recess in the brick, known as the 'frog'. These 'green bricks' were then placed on pallets, which were sent to the long open drying sheds for three to six weeks. A special press was used to extrude pipes for field drains.

Making roof tiles was a different process altogether, using clay in a drier state. The tiles were

Bill from Framlingham brickworks for the supply of gravel. In another bill for sand only, there is a charge of '6d extra when not using our bricks'.

not moulded but beaten over a shaped block using tools rather like small cricket bats. The final process was the firing, when it might take 2–3 days to load the kiln, with air gaps between each brick, to allow even circulation of the heat. To form the bricks from the moulded clay, a bright red heat was required with a temperature between 1,740 and 2,100°F. During the final stages, someone would usually remain on site at night to keep the fires stoked.

Smith's brickyard had two kilns, which could each hold 30,000 bricks, and take a week to fire. Two kilns would be necessary for a commercial brickworks, due to the time taken for loading, firing and striking the kiln, the whole process being very labour intensive. Decorative items such as the 'daisy rose' mould were also produced, and these can be seen on houses at the end of Station Road.

These rose-motif bricks can be seen on houses in Station Road, and were made in the nearby brickworks.

Land drains were often manufactured at the brickworks, using a press to extrude them. Location unknown.

Brickmaking itself ceased during the winter months, as frost would split the green bricks while they still had a high moisture content. The seasonal nature of this work could fit in well with that of malting, which was primarily a winter activity. The advent of cheap mass produced bricks eventually closed these small works, which were common throughout the country.

The Butcher

The butcher processed and sold a range of meat and poultry products. In the 1901 census there were nine separate butchers, either employing others or as sole traders. John Brownsord originally had his shop on the Market Hill, but these premises were taken over by Ben Durrant in about 1898. This was to be a typical business, being handed down through the generations, but it closed when Ben died prematurely in 1915 after he fell from a ladder and broke his neck. His brother Fred then carried on the trade from 1917, after which it passed to his nephew Fred and then Fred's son John.

Ben Durrant took over John Brownsord's shop on the Market Hill, next to the Queen's Head alley. In this photo is Fred Durrant who eventually continued the business after his brother's premature death in 1915. Note the traditional boater hat, along with delivery bicycle held by Sid Cotton.

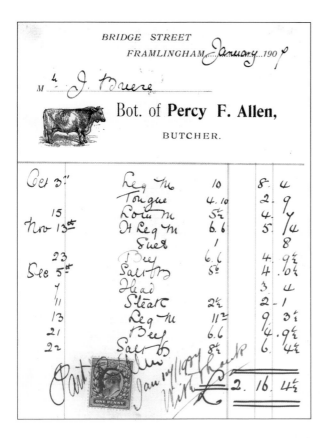

Head alley. This could hold up to three animals, which would be killed on the same day. The process was not for the faint hearted. A rope would be put around the bullock's head and then passed through a ring attached to a post. The beast would then be pulled against the post and despatched by a blow to the head with a poleaxe. Pigs had their throats cut.

Skill was required in processing the carcase in order to obtain the correct cuts of meat without wast-

The slaugh-terman would despatch the beast with a blow to the head with a poleaxe.

The butchers knew the local farmers well, and had informal arrangements to buy stock from them. Percy Allen, whose shop was in Bridge Street, was buying bullocks from James Breese for 7s 9d per stone, but this was offset against James' meat bill. Most of Durrant's meat came from Isaac Larter of Moat Farm, when the cattle would be driven along the road to the slaughterhouse in the Queen's

age. The meat was hung for about two weeks before being sold. The skins and hides were of value; they would be sold to the fellmonger, achieving a higher price if they were in good condition. Beef and pork were most favoured, with lamb less so.

Shooting was a very popular pursuit, and there was also a ready market for rabbits and pheasants.

One of the difficulties faced by the butcher and fishmonger was the preservation of their products

Displays such as this were limited to the cold winter months. In the summer, the butcher relied on a quick turnover of his meat as the use of ice was not practical at that time in rural areas. The steel hanging from the butcher's belt was to sharpen his knives. Kerridge's shop, Bridge Street, c. 1895.

in hot weather. Block ice imported from Norway was available in large ports and cities, but it was not a practical or economic option for the rural butcher until a later period when mechanical transport was available. Instead, he relied on a cool storeroom and a quick turnover in the summer months.

The butcher normally served a four year apprenticeship, and would proudly wear the boater hat and apron by which the trade was known. There might be up to half a dozen people employed, from the butcher himself down to the local delivery boy. Durrant had two horses and carts in use for delivering meat to their customers, who would pass on their next order at the same time.

Certain delicacies of the butcher have lost their appeal to today's customers. 'Pigs fry' consisted of the liver and heart which were very tasty when fried. Chitterlings were the pig intestines, which had to be washed several times, then soaked in salt water before boiling and straining, and were then eaten hot or cold. The intestine coverings were used for the sausage skins. Brains and tails were also cooked, while sweetbread was made from the pancreas or thymus gland of a calf. Offal and blood

were used to make black pudding, with blocks of lard being prepared from melted pig fat, and dripping from bullock fat. There was a steady demand for all such products, being cheaper than the main cuts of meat.

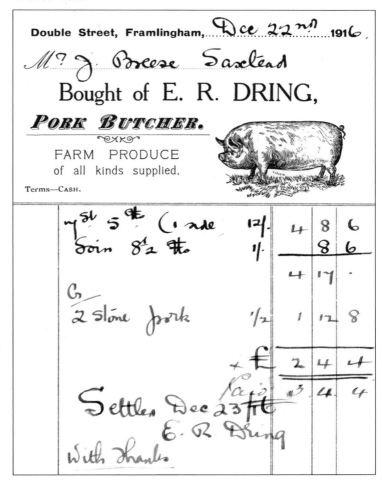

The importance of Double Street as a place of trade had declined, and by 1916 there were only about seven businesses. James Breese had been given credit in this account for two stone of pork to offset his bill.

Suffolk cured ham is still a special treat, and was produced by immersing the hindquarters of a pig in pickle for several days before being placed in a smokehouse. Oak shavings were mainly used for the smoking process, after which the ham was sewn into a muslin bag, and rubbed with salt before being hung until needed.

In addition to general butchers there were those who were solely pork butchers, such as George Canham in Fore Street and E. Dring in Double Street. There were always several butchers in any town, and competition between them was keen. A close check would be kept on each others' prices.

The processing of pigs and their curing was intended to become a large industry in Framlingham when Roe's Hygienic Company opened for business in 1898 in their old manure works at Broadwater. The press were treated to lunch at the Crown, followed by a conducted tour of the premises, but this was to be a short lived venture. It closed in 1900, when the Company's premises, which included the Mount Pleasant post mill, were sold at auction.

A rare account for the short-lived bacon factory. The telegram address of 'Rosebud' related to the name that Augustus Roe gave to his inventions, one being a device to allow meat pies to breathe. Any revenue from his inventions was not enough to prevent the factory closing within two years.

The Carpenter and Wheelwright

Wood has always been used in the construction of houses, barns, wagons and furniture, as well as the coffin for that final journey. The carpenter's knowledge and special tools were often handed down from one generation to the next. He could also buy tools in the town, the typical cost around 1900 being:

jack plane	5s 9d	smoothing plane	4s 3d
tenon saw	3s 3d	spokeshave	8d
pincers	1s 0d	screwdriver	1s 0d
gimlet	4d	bradawl	4d

It is also a trade which is just as important in the present century as it was in earlier times. Wood is still seen as the traditional material for good furniture and building fixtures, so the carpenter will be an important tradesman for the foreseeable future. The wheelwright has not been so fortunate in retaining his place in the community. The Leggetts had been wheelwrights in Double Street in the first half of the nineteenth century, and with Richard Leggett later in College Road. The business was

in due course carried on by John Moore, who married Richard's sister, and after his death in 1877 by Richard's sons Charles and Henry.

The wheelwright saw himself as more skilled than the carpenter. George Sturt's classic book

Wheelwright's shop, Hollesley, c.1900. The bowler-hatted man is using a jack plane.

The Wheelwright's Shop says that 'while any man able to make a wheel knew enough to be a carpenter, on the other hand a carpenter could not do wheelwright's work, for lack of apprenticeship'. The title of wheelwright is rather misleading as he was also responsible for making the whole cart or wagon. A bill of Moore's for 1912 shows '2 new tumbrels complete – £28'. There was of necessity a close working relationship with the blacksmith as a wheel could not be made without the co-operation of both trades.

The wheelwright would usually source the trees to be used, and remove the bark. If it was oak, the bark could be sold to the tanner. Large trunks could be moved over difficult ground using a timber jim, a clever arrangement consisting of an arched timber with a braced pole at right angles and a stout wooden wheel on each side. The jim would be placed over a log with one wheel on each side and stood up so that the pole was vertical. The log would then be chained to the upper part of the arched timber near its point of balance and the pole hauled down by a horse, the arched timber lifting the log as it turned towards a vertical position. The pole was then chained to the log, two or more horses were harnessed to the jim and away

The timber jim was a simple but effective device for pulling trees out of woodlands, as well as for haulage on the road. The log would be chained to it with the pulling beam in the upright direction. When pulled down, the offset position of the axle raised the log off the ground.

1896 bill for wooding up plough. This would be for making a new beam, to which all the other parts are attached. In another account, for 1912, two complete tumbrels have been supplied at a cost of £28.

FRAMLINGHAM. *Dec* 189 6

Mr Breese Saxtead

Dr. to H. & C. MOORE,

WHEELWRIGHTS · AND · CARPENTERS.

| Oct | *New Wooding up Plough* | 14 0 |

Settled Jany 30 1897

HC Moore

they went. An alternative carrier was the timber drug, which had four wheels and could carry more than one log, each one being loaded either by a tripod and lifting gear or by being rolled up ramps on to the drug.

The arduous task of sawing the wood then com-

This 1897 bill has several interesting items. The overhaul of a trap includes lining the wheels, repairs, painting, varnishing and oiling. There is also a separate sum of 9s 1d for ironwork from Bridges the blacksmith.

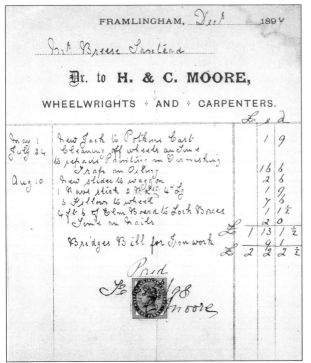

menced. The pit saw only cut on the downward stroke, and the bottom sawyer was subject to all the sawdust, debris and heat that accumulated in his below ground pit. The logs were held in place with metal 'dogs'.

The expression 'top dog' derives from the higher status of the top sawyer who guided the saw, while the bottom sawyer's role was to pull down on the cutting stroke. The sawing process would sometimes be performed by an outside team of sawyers,

Alfred Andrews was an apprentice carpenter at Snape Maltings c.1890. He is holding a bow saw.

who later on might progress to a mobile steam powered saw mill. The sawn timber would then be stacked with strips of wood between the planks to allow ventilation, often for many years. Smyth's of Peasenhall used no ash for wheel felloes that had not been stacked for fourteen years.

Great skill was needed in the construction of the wheel, not least in the selection of suitable timber, typically with oak for the spokes, ash for the felloes (pronounced fellies, the rim sections), beech or ash for the axle arms, and elm for the hub. Iron axle arms from specialist suppliers were bolted to the wooden axle, and were in common use by the end of the nineteenth century, replacing the earlier all wooden type. The wagon wheel is dished, so that spokes are vertical when they take the load to the ground, which leads to the top of the wheel sloping outwards. The technical reasons for the dished wheel were often disputed between wheelwrights, but from a practical point of view allowed a wider body and prevented mud and water falling directly onto the hub, and countered the sway induced by the movement of the horse.

Apart from wheels and wagons, the wheelwright would also make wheelbarrows and ladders. The latter would require poles of the necessary length, tapering in diameter to about 2½ inches at the top. They would be sawn in two, and holes bored for the staves, which were made of oak, using a draw knife. The ladder was then assembled with wooden wedges driven into the staves.

The services of the wheelwright were less in demand as pneumatic tyres on steel rims became more common, but as an accomplished worker in wood his skills would always be in demand. Moore Brothers were still listed as wheelwrights in 1937, although they had also been undertakers for many years by then. Good quality coffins were usually made from one inch thick oak or elm. The shaped side was achieved by a series of cross cuts to the inner face of the plank, which was then heated by boiling water until the correct angle was achieved. Moore's also built the current bier, which is used to take the coffin from the cemetery gates to the graveside. Their trade subsequently diversified into that of building contractors.

Carpenters such as Tom Dale on the Market Hill could turn their skills to the manufacture of household furniture as well as doors and sash windows etc. The glue used in the frames was derived from animal bones, another good example of recycled products.

For a picture of the interior of a wheelwright's shop, see page 189.

The Carter and Carrier

The hard labour on the farms and the range of trades within the town all generated goods which needed to reach a more distant market. There was also a need for those in rural areas to visit the market town. Most people could not afford the considerable cost of owning horse drawn transport, and in 1900 the motor bus was still a few years away.

It was the carrier who provided a service that passed through many towns and villages with pick up points, normally an inn, on specific days and times. In 1900, there were seven different carriers whose routes took them through Framlingham. The main pick up points were the Crown Hotel, Station Hotel and Railway Inn, with destinations to most of the surrounding villages, and Ipswich twice a week. William Meen's last departure from the Crown Hotel was at 6 p.m. for Stradbroke, which must have been a tiresome journey in the winter months.

The carrier's cart was fairly basic, some being fully exposed to the elements, while others were enclosed. They had hard wooden seats that ran from front to back on either side. Passengers would face each other over the long bumpy journey, with all the packages piled up on the floor between them, along with any small livestock for the market. The carrier would also take orders from customers along the route, to buy goods on their behalf in the town, an important service that would avoid them making the trip in person.

Warrenton Page in his book on Holbrook, refers to William Stiff the local carrier. He would sound the bugle about 9 a.m., when the passengers would ready themselves for the six mile journey into Ipswich. Their arrival was nearly two hours later, and for that reason others would get him to buy

The carrier provided an important service between town and village, for goods and passengers. Charles Mayhew operated from Ipswich, c.1912. After the war, ex-War Department lorries started to take over from the slower pace of the horse drawn era.

Businesses which manufactured goods usually had their own transport. These wagons are hauled by a 1919 Garrett 4 CD steam tractor belonging to Barnard and Middleton of Badingham brickworks. They were also haulage contractors. The location is the Haynings in Framlingham, with Clarke's malting/seed store to the right. The wagons are full of coal, en route to the brick kilns.

goods on their behalf. One woman even trusted him to buy her corsets!

The carter would be contracted to collect and deliver goods, either on a regular or one-off basis.

The corn merchant and miller, for example, would have their own horses and wagons, for deliveries were an integral part of their trade. The Great Eastern Railway appointed Robert Scoggins as their carrier in 1894, but in later years the service was run by the railway's own carters. In 1901 there were 20 people in Framlingham who were classified in the census as carters.

There would also be businesses which either set up as carters or offered the service as a sideline. The ownership of horses and stabling costs were always considerable, so it was important to keep them in profitable work as much as possible.

William Hatcher started as a coal merchant in Station Road in 1902. He was soon advertising as a carrier to Hacheston, and in 1906 moved to College Road, where he would eventually operate mainly as a carter. It was Mr Hatcher's horses that were used to pull the fire engine. If a fire occurred at night, the black horses had to be rounded up in the dark from the meadow where they were kept; but that's another story. As the business grew, he moved to larger

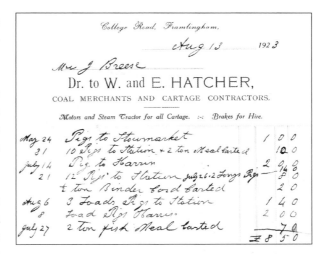

ABOVE: *Horses, steam and motors were all available in 1923. This bill includes trips to the Harris bacon factory in Ipswich, along with carting binder cord and fish meal.*

BELOW: *G. G. Whorlow of Sudbury, with an impressive display of horse-drawn delivery vehicles.*

premises in Badingham Road from about 1930, and traded along with his wife Ellen as W. & E. Hatcher. He bought the Pound Farm buildings, where the original pound for the enclosure of stray or wild animals still existed. The field opposite would later become the Pageant Field, and Hatcher also built a house and workshops on the road frontage.

In the 1920s he was able to offer 'motors', and 'steam tractors' for carting, along with horse drawn 'brakes' for hire. He also expanded into contract threshing, with two Clayton and Shuttleworth threshing tackles and straw pitchers, powered by Garrett engines. The use of horses, steam power and motors conjures up a nostalgic scene that would have been relatively short lived.

In later years, the emphasis was on lorries for livestock and general haulage, along with coal delivery. There were eight cattle lorries, and a further two for the sugar beet season. A common destination was the Harris bacon factory in Ipswich, but on occasions a much longer journey to their Calne factory in Wiltshire. There was regular work to the cattle markets, with Wickham Market on Monday, Ipswich on Tuesday, Saxmundham and Halesworth on alternate Wednesdays, along with Bury St Edmunds and Stowmarket on Thursday and Diss on Friday.

The massive lorries on our roads today are the modern embodiment of the carter, and they have mainly recaptured the routes that were gained by the railways in the nineteenth century, and lost again to Dr Beeching's axe in the twentieth century.

Harry Flemming with Ford Model T lorry outside Hatcher's College Road premises.

The Chemist and Druggist

When illness occurred in most homes, the traditional remedies were tried before a visit to the chemist was considered. A direct call to the doctor would only be for those who could afford his services, which did not apply to the working person off sick and receiving no pay.

The chemist sold proprietary chemical based products whereas the druggist provided animal and herbal based medicines which were probably little different from the home remedy. Laudanum was made from morphine dissolved in alcohol, and was sold as a solution that could be taken on its own, or mixed with wine or water. The alcohol content enabled the morphine to enter the blood stream swiftly, resulting in a speedy feeling of euphoria. It was often mixed with syrup and used as a 'quietening' mixture for children. Opium collected from poppy capsules contains several alkaloids, the main one of which is morphine.

James Hulland's chemist shop was on the corner of Market Hill and Church Lane, where he manufactured his Balsam of Tolu and Iceland Moss, as a universal remedy for coughs and colds. He claimed that it would 'produce expectoration, gently excite

perspiration and allay irritation of the mucous membrane'. This was also sold through agents in the county and in London. Other remedies included chilblain ointment, Dentine for tooth ache and dandelion pills for liver complaints. There

JAMES HULLAND,

CHEMIST,

MARKET HILL, ☙ **FRAMLINGHAM.**

COUGHS!   COUGHS!

All those afflicted with the above complaint should try

Hulland's Balsam of Tolu and Iceland Moss,

which will be found a speedy and effectual remedy. For Coughs, Colds, Bronchitis, Asthma, and all affections of the Chest and Lungs it stands unequalled. Its action is to produce expectoration, gently excite perspiration, and allay irritation of the mucous membrane. It is an excellent remedy for Whooping Cough, and from its agreeable taste and the fact that it contains no opiate, may be given with perfect safety to children. In Bottles, 1/1½, 2/9, 4/6.

CHILBLAIN OINTMENT.

A new remedy for this troublesome complaint. No irksome rubbing as with most remedies. After a few applications with a camel's hair brush all irritation is allayed.   Sold in Bottles 7½d., 1/1½.

PAINT FOR CORNS AND WARTS.

A Painless and Effectual Cure for Hard and Soft Corns, Warts. Is not poison and does not irritate. Sold in Bottles, 7½d., 1/1½, free per post.

DENTINE.

The INSTANT CURE FOR TOOTHACHE. A few drops on wool relieves the pain and prevents extraction. Bottles, 1/- free per post.

DANDELION PILLS.

A Stimulant to the Liver without mercury. These Pills will be found to be one of the best remedies for a Weak Stomach, Impaired Digestion, and all Disorders of the Liver.   In Boxes, 1/1½, 2/9.

HULLAND'S LITTLE LIVER PILLS

Are a Cure for Torpid Liver, and Cure Bilious Headaches without fail. 1/1½ Per Box.

Agents for the above:—
Aldeburgh-on-Sea   ...   Mr. F. T. COOPER.
Leiston   ...   ...   Mr. T. P. GOOCH.

James Hulland's shop was on the corner of Church Lane and Market Hill and offered a cure for every ailment.

were also many nationally advertised products such as 'Clarke's World Famous Blood Mixture', which was claimed to cleanse the blood from all impurities from whatever cause arising. There was inevitably a ready market for such products.

The Victorian chemist's shop sold a wide range of goods, including hair dressings (macassor oil), dyes, soaps, tooth powder, bed pans, along with the less obvious such as spices, tea, ink, candles, lamp oil, cigarettes and eventually petrol. Betts' Market Hill shop encouraged you to buy your surgical appliances from them, such as a double truss for 5s 0d, to save the exorbitant charges of the doctors. The Pharmacy Act of 1868 stated that all newcomers to the profession who wished to practice were required to pass examinations, whether or not they intended to become a member of the Pharmaceutical Society. They would then be able to dispense various chemicals including scheduled poisons which were sold in green bottles. Reginald Betts' accounts proudly proclaim that he is a 'dispensing chemist by examination'.

Large coloured glass carboys were often displayed in the windows, with powders and herbs stored in jars and drawers. Towards the end of the Victorian

period, a far greater range of medicines was available. Specie jars and the smaller 'shop rounds' were used to store them, while the carboys were increasingly for display purposes only. The simplest medicines were originally sold as powders

Betts advertisement of 1896 showing the wide range of products available. The concept of mixing paint colours in the shop is not new.

REGINALD BETTS,
Agricultural Chemist,
OIL, COLOUR & PETROLEUM MERCHANT,
— MARKET HILL, —
FRAMLINGHAM.

BETTS' CONDITION POWDERS for HORSES
1/- and 2/- Tins.

BETTS' COUGH POWDERS,
1/- and 1/2 dozen, for Horses and Cattle.

BETTS' CONDITION BALLS, 3/- dozen.

BETTS' COUGH BALLS, 2/- dozen.

BETTS' GRIPE DRINKS, 1/6 each, 15/- dozen.

The above are all Manufactured from the old recipes of the late John Betts, M R.C.V.S., of Woodbridge, and were employed by him for over 50 years in an extensive practice; they are confidently recommended to all Horse and Cattle Keepers or Rearers, as safe, *effectual*, and cheap.

Special Agent for all Gostling & Co.'s Diss Preparations, Thorley's Food, Simpson's Spice and Calf Meal at lowest prices.

LARD OIL & MACHINE OILS, LINSEED OIL & TURPENTINE.

Every shade and description of
PAINTS, ENAMELS, VARNISHES, &c.

N.B.—Paint mixed to match any shade of paper, wood, or old paint work.

RIGHT: These ornate storage jars are from Stearn, the chemist in Stowmarket. Although the application of leeches might seem outdated, they are still used, for example in reconstructive surgery when problems occur due to blood congestion. The leech's saliva anaesthetises the wound, fights blood clots and assists blood flow to the veins.

wrapped in paper, and often tasted unpleasant. It was a common belief that a medicine would do you no good if it did not taste nasty. The powder could be mixed with liquorice and glucose to form a pliable mix, which was then used to make pills. The pestle, mortar and pill making machine were essential parts of the chemist's equipment.

William Manning was a chemist and druggist in 1820, eventually moving from Double Street to the Market Hill, which has been the location for such shops ever since. The business of chemist was one which lent itself to expansion in other towns. Gostling, for example, had their main outlet in Diss, and by 1900 had branches in Pulham Market, Eye, Debenham and on the Market Hill in Framlingham. This is the same location as the present chemist. Despite several changes of ownership, these premises have been in continuous use for that purpose for over 110 years.

In rural areas the chemist also catered for farm animals, with Gostling advertising horse, cattle, sheep and pig medicines. This carried on well into the twentieth century, as C. H. Stevens was still offering veterinary and agricultural preparations in the 1950s. By that time, though, the photographic side had increased and today the chemist still provides a wide range of goods, although you may have trouble finding horse balls.

Herbert Sara was manager of Gostling's chemist shop on the Market Hill and took over the business in 1912.

Communications

The commercial life of a town is very dependent on its ability to communicate with suppliers and customers. The Post Office had been in various locations before the current purpose built office in Riverside opened in 1903. From around 1890 there were three deliveries each day, at 7.00 a.m. and 9.00 a.m., and 6.30 p.m., while the post office remained open until 8.00 p.m. on weekdays. The present post boxes in College Road and Double Street were installed in 1883. Their design dates back to 1856, with the early form of vertical posting slot, and would have been in use elsewhere before starting their long period of service in Framlingham. The first pillar box in Britain was set up in Jersey in 1852. This was from a recommendation by Anthony Trollope the novelist, who was at the time a surveyor's clerk for the Post Office. Letters not exceeding 4 oz in weight could be posted for 1d. Postcards with an imprinted ½d stamp were introduced in 1870, but it was the ability to affix adhesive stamps from 1894 that popularised this form of communication.

Alfred Kerridge became a postman in 1915 at 16 years of age, and for a year delivered the post to

Alfred (Bo) Kerridge in his postal uniform, 1915. He lost his arm in the First World War, but went on to deliver the post in Framlingham throughout his working life.

Badingham. Then, along with many of his friends, he joined the army to fight in France. A brief account of his experience needs to be told, as it portrays the combination of horror and humanity that existed together. On his nineteenth birthday, only two months before the end of the war, a shell explosion blew him into a crater. On coming to, he

found that his arm was missing, and that he was sharing the crater with a German whose leg had been blown off. The enemy soldier made a tourniquet for his leg from scraps of wood and rope, and then indicated to Alfred that he would do the same for his arm, which he did. They were eventually found and taken to a Red Cross Hospital. After the war, it was thought unlikely that he would be able to continue his work as a postman. However, the postmaster was determined that he should do so,

and Alfred Kerridge, commonly called 'Bo', was to become a familiar face around the town for many years until he retired aged 62.

Telegraphic communication was in existence to the station from its opening in 1859. Before 1868,

Henry Damant held the post office in Albert Place in 1900, and employed two telegraph operators. The insulators for the telegraph wires are just visible on the corner of the building at roof level.

the systems had been operated by the railway and private telegraph companies. The Telegraph Bill of that year was the first time the government had taken over a private enterprise, which would be run by the Post Office. With the emphasis on service rather than profit, this allowed the telegraph to be extended, and in rural areas brought to all Money Order offices.

The charge introduced in 1870 was for a tariff of one shilling for a 20-word message, with 3*d* for each additional five words. Within two years of the new Bill, the telegraph had reached Richard Green's post office in Church Street. From there it moved to Henry Damant's shop in Albert Place, where he employed two telegraph operators. This was to remain an important means of providing a rapid printed message, often covering goods to be ordered from local businesses. In 1885, the tariff was reduced to 6*d* for 12 words or less, plus ½*d* for any extra words. Although this provided an efficient means of commercial communication, it was little used by the public. In 1900, a letter could be delivered at a postage cost of 1*d*, compared with 6*d* for the telegram. The Wheatstone and Morse code system was used by the telegraph operators for many years to send the messages. It was not until the 1930s that the teleprinter was in common use to provide a print-out that could be directly read by the recipient. By that time, the telegraph was losing out to the increased convenience of the telephone for commercial use.

The first public telephone exchange opened in this country in 1879, but it would be nearly 30 years before Framlingham had its own exchange, which

A telegraphist sending a message using a single needle instrument, c.1912. The Morse code was transmitted using two keys. One was pressed to send a dot, the other a dash. On receiving a message, deflections of the needle, which can be clearly seen, indicated left for dot, and right for dash. Central Telegraph Office, London.

opened for business at the new Riverside post office on 30th May 1908, when Frederick Ling the solicitor took the first call. All calls had to be connected by the local operator, which restricted the hours of use. By 1923, the service was still only available from 8.00 a.m. to 9.30 p.m. on weekdays, and 9.00 a.m. to 10.30 a.m. on Sunday. The take up of the new communication system was slow. At the outset there were 13 subscribers, which by 1923 had only increased to about 30. The telephone exchange moved in 1926 to the front room of a residential house, Glenview, in Fore Street, where Mrs Shemming was the operator.

Private telephones had been used before then for communication over a short distance. For example, Frederick Button at Mount Pleasant had two Byng telephones complete with microphones, call bells, induction coils and wiring installed between his house and the mill in 1903.

Appendix 4 provides a list of subscribers based on the telephone directory of 1923, along with earlier numbers from local invoices. A few numbers did change within this period. The *East Anglian Daily Times* in 1922 reported a general outcry against the high cost of making use of the telephone, and was thankful that directories would in future be available at a lower price.

By 1930, the number of subscribers had crept up to 50 with the connection of Framlingham College. The Station was No. 43, while the Saxtead Call Office was No. 46. Mabel Gladwell took over as chief operator after her mother's death in 1936, and the exchange remained there until 1961.

Operator seated at a 100-line magneto telephone exchange c.1900. When the Framlingham exchange opened in 1908, calls could only be made between 8.00 a.m. and 9.30 p.m. on weekdays, and for 1½ hours on a Sunday. There were only 13 subscribers.

The Corn Merchant

The harvest yield and the price of corn would determine whether it would be a good year for the farmer, which had a knock on effect with local tradesmen. It was the corn merchant who struck a deal with the farmer, and paid him for the goods. As the quantities of wheat and barley increased in the mid-nineteenth century, a more efficient means of conducting business was established and, in line with most towns, a corn exchange was built. This was incorporated within the Crown Hotel and opened in 1847 with stands for 30 members.

Bury St Edmunds had the main East Anglian corn market, but in an age before the motor car, the small corn exchange was an important place of business. The merchant would usually have an order, perhaps from a brewer or maltings, and he

The horse and cart were the mainstay for transporting small loads to and from the merchant or miller.

would expect to fill that order from his many familiar customers when they visited his stand.

Some millers, such as Thomas Buckmaster of Victoria Mill, were also corn merchants, but others specialised and developed into large businesses, with the railway station being a focal point. Alfred Creasy started as a corn and coal merchant in the 1860s. In 1892, Herbert Manby was taken into the partnership, and in 1900 took over the company, which traded as Herbert Manby & Co. The corn would be collected from the farms, and matched with other batches before being delivered to local millers/maltsters or loaded on to the rail wagons. A coomb sack of wheat weighed 18 stone, and with beans nearly 19 stone

Larger loads were delivered by horse and wagon. Fred Banthorpe is at the head of Frederick Cooke's team from Saxtead Lodge, at the Framlingham Horse Show, 1903.

robust vehicles were needed. Manby bought a 1912 five-ton Garrett steam wagon for the purpose, but prior to that the horse and wagon were used. Harry Walne became a director of that company, which bore his name from 1939, when Herbert Manby died. However, it was Edwin George Clarke who founded the company that would eventually become the largest employer in Framlingham. On his arrival from Worlingworth in 1879 he started as a maltster, but soon widened his interests to include trading in corn, coal and coke. The business grew, with buildings along Station Road, having their own rail siding *(see the map on page 147)*. Borrowing money to purchase grain was not always easy and his son Percy recalled his father sending him to organise a loan.

Herbert Manby's 1912 Garrett five-ton steam wagon in Riverside, with Fred Finbow the driver, next to the cab. Drawing by John Western from original photograph. Note water pump to the right, which still exists.

He was swiftly dismissed by the bank manager, and instructed to tell his father that he must learn to cut his coat according to his cloth.

There were several corn merchants in Framlingham, and the farmer would be intent on gaining the best price from them. In 1900, typical prices obtained by James Breese were as follows:

39 coombs of barley to Mr Manby
      at 14*s* 0*d* per coomb
47 coombs of wheat to Mr Maulden (miller)
      at 13*s* 6*d* per coomb
25 coombs of wheat to Mr Clarke
      at 13*s* 3*d* per coomb.

Two of E. G. Clarke's sons, Percy (Colonel E. P.) and Hugh, joined the firm, which saw great expansion during the 1920s and 30s. A train with eight fully loaded trucks would be despatched each day to a distant maltings. All such orders were personally negotiated at the buyers' premises, which might be in Burton on Trent, Leeds, Newcastle or other remote locations.

Corn was mainly purchased at the local markets, and John Hewitt describes in his book *Two Horse Power* the general activity in the Ipswich Corn Exchange.

> There was a deep-noted buzz: it was impossible to hear what anybody said unless you stood quite close together. The busiest place was the stand belonging to Colonel Clarke of Framlingham.

A typical busy Tuesday at Ipswich Corn Exchange, where Colonel E. P. Clarke conducted much business. This scene would have changed little over time. The only stand sign readily identifiable is W. Ladbrook and Son, of Elmsett.

The Colonel and Joe Peck would be surrounded by men with samples. Their samples came mostly in blue sugar-paper bags. Joe would usually have the first look, pour some into one hand and put his nose right into the grains. If there was the slightest suspicion of a smell, he returned the sample to its owner.

When Joe deemed a sample acceptable, he passed it to the Colonel, who would put some grain in a hand held device with a blade which, when the lid was closed, sheared the grains in half. The price was mainly determined by the colour. A grey colour was of limited value, while strong white would achieve the highest price for malting barley. The lower grades would be sold to the farmer as feed for livestock. Bury St Edmunds (Wednesday) and Norwich (Saturday) were the busiest corn markets in East Anglia, along with Ipswich (Tuesday) and Beccles (Friday). The peak period of trade was from September through to March.

Percy Clarke would catch the train on Monday from Framlingham to visit the London Corn Exchange at Mark Lane. It was not unknown for the train to be held for him, if he was delayed. The trading process was reversed at Mark Lane, as he was selling and not buying.

The corn merchant often dealt in other goods, such as coal, fertiliser, salt and seed grain, as well as animal feed. The latter would become a large part of his trade, which initially started in the old black granary building at the station, where two millstones were driven by horse power. The business of E. G. Clarke started in a very small way in 1879 and grew to become the largest East Anglian barley merchant by the late 1930s. Post war trading saw increased competition, bulk movement of grain, and supplies being sourced from other areas. Before then, the brewers had favoured barley from the eastern counties.

E. G. Clarke 1899 account for maize, oats, fish salt and superphosphate. There is a charge of two shillings for transport (porterage), and a cheque provided for £5 18s 0d, to balance exactly the sum paid for wheat purchased from James Breese.

The Doctor

A visit by the doctor was reserved for serious illness or accidents, since a bill was normally received for his services. If you were a servant, your employer was expected to pay these bills, or if you had joined a friendly society, they would meet medical expenses in a time of need. The very poor might gain treatment under the Poor Law Reform Act of 1834, when the surgeon was paid by the Poor Law Union, provided the relieving officer considered it an appropriate case.

Dr Cordy Jeaffreson's printed bill for professional services shows that they were issued annually.

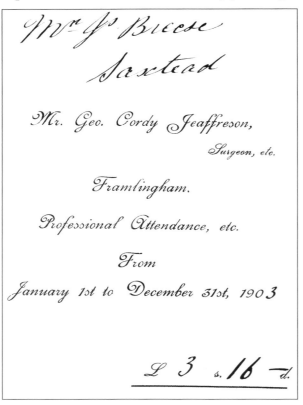

Nurse Ada Hart, 1902. A doctor would invariably work on his own in a small town, and a patient would only see a uniformed nurse if they needed hospital treatment.

The surname Jeaffreson was linked with the medical profession in Framlingham for nearly 100 years. In 1836, William Jeaffreson became the first man in England to successfully remove an ovarian cyst by operation. He was elected as a Fellow of the Royal College of Surgeons in 1844. Before the introduction of anaesthesia and antisepsis in the late nineteenth century, such operations were attended with considerable risk, and most people were terrified of the surgeon's knife. Ann Bridges had an abscess on her knee which failed to clear up. The ensuing infection eventually meant that amputation was the only option. Her death certificate states she refused amputation over a period of many weeks, and eventually died in 1856.

One of William Jeaffreson's sons, George Edwards Jeaffreson, served the town for over 40 years, and in 1895 was President of the East Anglian Branch of the British Medical Association. He had a very practical approach to situations, as witnessed by the parents of a young boy who had consumption (tuberculosis). Jeaffreson told them on several occasions to leave the bedroom window open for ventilation. Finding it closed on his next visit, he kicked out the window frame! When he died in 1911, his son George Cordy Jeaffreson was in practice. He was the first person in Framlingham to own a motor car.

The first examination for general practitioners

Dr Nicholson in a Rover car outside his surgery at The Limes in College Road. He was a surgeon in the town between 1904 and 1910. The car was a great benefit to the doctor, but unreliability could be a problem.

was the Apothecaries Act of 1815. Following five years with a surgeon, and 15 months walking the wards of a teaching hospital, he would become a Licentiate of the Society of Apothecaries (LSA). The Medical Registration Act was passed in 1858, and it was generally accepted that properly educated G.P.s would become members of the Royal College of Surgeons, as well as having the LSA. Dr George Cordy Jeaffreson (1865–1930) was a Licentiate of the Royal College of Physicians, a Member of the Royal College of Surgeons and a Licentiate of the Society of Apothecaries, these being standard qualifications for a doctor of his era.

The life of a doctor in a place such as Framlingham would have been better than in a new practice in a larger town or city. In our period, there was an excess of doctors, which often meant a poor living from fees, unless you were well established or inherited a practice. A doctor's income mainly derived from the fees charged for visits, maternity cases and the sale of medicines, along with appointments to businesses, local authorities and schools etc. The list below shows such appointments in 1900:

George Robert Adcock – Age 33, of College Road. MRCS, LRCP. Medical Officer to Framlingham College, Hoxne Union (District 4 & 6), and the Great Eastern Railway Framlingham area.

Joseph Bowerman Drew – Age 44, of The Haynings. LRCP&S. Edinburgh. Medical Officer and public vaccinator, Framlingham district Plomesgate Union.

George Cordy Jeaffreson – Age 31, of Market Hill. LRCP, MRCS, LSA.

George Edwards Jeaffreson – Age 65, of Moat House. JP, MRCS, LSA.

A typical small-town doctor worked on his own, with his wife often providing essential back-up services. A room in his house would be the surgery, with patients possibly waiting in the dining room. The level of expectation from the patient was not that high, usually satisfied by some form of medicine which was dispensed by the doctor and not the chemist. Physical examination was not necessarily the norm, particularly in the case of female patients, and diagnostic equipment was often limited to a stethoscope and thermometer. Doctors would need to treat most conditions. They would stitch wounds, lance boils, set broken bones, deliver babies and occasionally amputate limbs. The doctor would also be the dentist, and when teeth had been removed, the patients could visit Eustace Gibbs in Fore Street, who was a manufacturer of artificial teeth. Conditions such as measles, scarlet fever and tuberculosis were often fatal, there being no effective treatment at the time. To cope with his work, the doctor needed to be tough and resourceful, and usually available at all times.

Perhaps the most famous son of Framlingham was Henry Thompson (1820-1904), who worked in his father's grocery shop on the Market Hill until entering medical school at the age of twenty seven. He then trained in London and later operated for a bladder stone on King Leopold of the Belgians, and similarly on Napoleon III. He was also founder of the Cremation Society, which met with much opposition – the first cremation did not take place until 1885. Sir Henry Thompson did not practise in Framlingham, but led a life in the high society of London. The church clock was provided by him in 1872 in memory of his father.

Domestic service

Before the era of universal domestic appliances, the everyday tasks in the more prosperous households were performed by any number of servants. Labour was cheap and there were few local opportunities for girls, so many took employment as general servants, housekeepers and companions. This general group represented the major source of employment in Framlingham, occupying a quarter of the whole work force. Inevitably most were employed by the head of the household, but the exception was that of the laundress or washerwoman, where half of them were self employed.

This was hard work, with the clothing being agitated by hand in a washing tub by the use of a wooden dolly, which had the appearance of a four or five legged stool with a large handle through the centre. Proprietary washing powders were available. The washing would then be rubbed up and down on a ribbed scrubbing board, prior to being boiled in the copper with soda and soap.

A quarter of the town's working population were in domestic service, being the main opportunity for female work. Most were employed, with the washerwoman being an exception, often working on her own account. The uniform of the average domestic worker was less fancy than that of the maids in the large house. It was usually limited to some form of pinafore.

This was then followed by three rinsing sessions. The mangle to remove excess water was an important part of the late Victorian household, and was an early concession to the mechanisation which would eventually revolutionise wash day. When the clothes were dry, they were ironed with the flat iron, which was heated on the stove. Box irons were also available, where a triangular shape of cast iron was heated in the fire, and then placed in the box of the iron. Coal or charcoal could also be used in the same way. The whole laundry process was arduous, and no easy way to make money.

Horse-drawn transport (seen here at the entrance to Fairfield House) lasted well into the twentieth century, ensuring work for groom and ostler.

Large country houses used to employ many servants, but numbers declined after World War 1. These maids worked at Brandeston Hall, c.1909.

'Monthly nurse' was a description often seen in the census, which referred to a nurse who attended a mother for the month following delivery of her baby.

The motor age had hardly reached Framlingham by 1900, so there were still grooms and ostlers to look after the horses. Ostlers were employed by the hotels and inns, and a faded sign for 'good stabling' can still be seen outside the Station Hotel. Until 1937, the employer needed to have a licence for a male servant, at the annual cost of 15 shillings.

Families were often large in number, irrespective of whether they were poor or well off. The old age pension was not introduced until 1909, when five shillings a week was provided to those at least 70 years old. Before then an extended family close by was the traditional way of looking after the elderly. If less fortunate, you would need to work for as long as possible, and one 78 year old widow was still employed as a char woman or general cleaner.

People normally worked for as long as they were able, unless they were fortunate enough to have saved enough through a well paid job or business.

A man such as E. G. Clarke had a cook and general servant, whereas the Duke of Hamilton on his large estate at Easton Park employed 23 people in the house alone during the 1880s, mostly recruited from far afield to limit the spread of local gossip.

Although domestic wages were low, the employment of servants was diminishing. There were the in-built costs of providing food and accommodation unless they lived near by. Also, those who did live in often resented the loss of freedom this incurred.

By the turn of the century, the number of young girls in service had fallen, as there were new opportunities if they were prepared to move. In large towns such as Ipswich, there were factory jobs which paid better wages, and provided more independence. William Pretty's corset factory, for example, had a nursery in 1904, and employed around 1,500 people by 1907. The Gurteen textile factories in Haverhill also employed large numbers of women, but such opportunities were not usually available in smaller towns and rural areas. Most married women with children were therefore still constrained to some form of domestic work.

Servants in the 1901 Framlingham census

	Number	Age Range
Charwoman	11	14–78
Coachman	3	39–42
Companion	5	22–59
Cook	14	17–33
Errand boy/girl	7	13–14
Gardener	12	16–74
General Servant	85	12–70
Groom/Ostler	14	18–53
Housekeeper	37	18–70
Housemaid	18	14–37
Laundress	22	19–66
Mother's help	6	17–45
Nurse	16	14–74

There was inevitably some overlap in the job descriptions, and the title given may not always be a true reflection of the work.

Gardener or general labourer, late 1920s. His general appearance (apart from the water-boots) is that of an earlier period. The wheelbarrow is a fine example of the wheelwright's craft.

The Draper and Outfitter

Outfitters, along with grocers, were the first trades to operate from a dedicated shop, and the early directories show 'shopkeepers' as a specific category. It was more usual to have some form of craft workshop, from which the manufactured goods would also be sold.

The draper and grocer were often the same person in trade directories of the 1850 period. By the turn of the twentieth century, there were several drapers in Framlingham. John Self took over the established business of Clodd and Larner in 1884, from premises in Well Close Square. Market Hill was the prime trad-

ing location, along with Double Street, although the latter is now almost exclusively residential.

Hatsell Garrard was a grocer and draper who had extensive premises on Market Hill, and was in business for many years before retiring in 1892, when George Jude took over. He traded as a silk mercer, hosier, haberdasher, dressmaker and milliner, as well as grocer, tea dealer and provision merchant. In addition, he sold carpets and lino, and provided a complete 'funeral service' with broughams, horses and a glass panelled carriage. It was not unusual for an outfitter to provide such a service, which could include the black outfits and handkerchiefs, along with black edged writing paper, envelopes and sealing wax. George died in 1899, and his wife Frances continued to trade for

Tweed cloth on display outside John Self's shop in Well Close Square. His interest in photography has left us with an important record of the town.

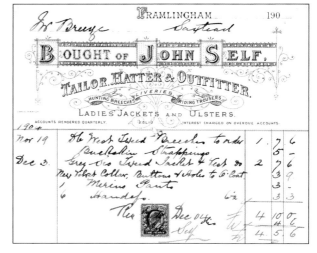

Aubrey Wicks acquired Stephen Starling's drapery shop in 1903, and developed it into a substantial business.

George Cooper had premises on the Market Hill, near to the Queen's Head alley. The hunting coat of best quality cloth cost three guineas, which was equivalent to about five weeks' wages for a farm worker in 1910.

a few years. The size of the business can be gauged by the fact that twelve assistants, mainly associated with the drapery trade, lived on the premises in 1901, as well as the family and domestic staff. It then passed to Barnes (1905), Addy (1910) and Wareing (1911), before the buildings were converted to A. G. Potter's car showrooms in 1930.

Another Market Hill draper was Stephen Starling, whose London House business was acquired by Aubrey Wicks in 1903 and became the largest such

Interior of Baker's drapery shop, Sudbury, c.1905.

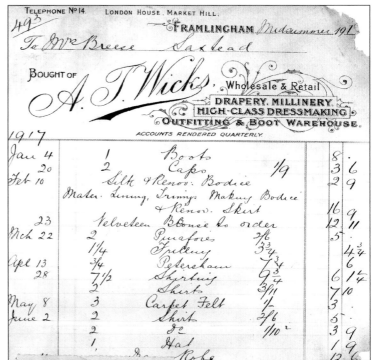

outlet in the town. He also had a boot warehouse which would have been in direct competition with Coleman's more traditional boot shop, located directly opposite.

The custom of well off patrons was sought, with references to 'high class dressmaking' and 'stylish millinery'. A typical shirt cost four shillings, and had detachable collars. These collars were changed each day whereas the shirt was not, a custom that has thankfully died out.

Such businesses had a large established range of customers but, in later years, access to the bus or motor car would allow a much wider choice of clothing to be seen, in Ipswich for example, which eventually precipitated the demise of many such shops.

The promotion of services with special offers is nothing new. Channing Dowsing was a tailor in Double Street, and his 1902 offer was that for every ten suit orders he received, he would refund the cost of one of them, by means of a draw. If you were in the market for a suit, this would have been tempting, as the cost varied between 27 and 38 shillings.

A market town served a large rural population, and

At a time when everyone wore a hat, there were plenty of opportunities for the milliner, and many were self employed. Read's shop was in Bridge Street, next to the river, between 1898 and 1906.

there was a need for a wide range of clothing suitable for work and recreation in the country. Freeman in Church Street took over from George Fisk in 1903 and advertised as 'The Shop For The Working Man'. They continued to provide that service well into the second part of the twentieth century.

The horseman on the farm took great pride in his own appearance as well as the turn out of his horses. Sam Friend (born 1888) of Framsden was such a horseman and recalled that a suit of clothes

would cost him five guineas at a time when his wages were ten shillings a week. He also had a coat made for himself, which over 50 years later, he considered was as good as when he bought it. When Paul Heiney wanted such a suit in the 1980s, it was retired tailor Bob Plant from Framlingham who was the only person able to help. He provided all the details for the flap pockets, drop falls and triple stitching etc. of the heavy tweed fabric which were necessary for a Suffolk suit.

Ten per cent of the workforce in Framlingham were involved with the drapery and clothing trade, with many being self-employed dressmakers, tailors and milliners. People did not usually venture far from home without some form of headwear,

and it was the milliner who made hats, mainly for women. Although ready made clothing was available, traditions changed slowly and many women in the town were able to offer dressmaking services from their homes. Extensive measurements were taken, which were then turned into a paper pattern. A toile was then cut from the pattern using a cheap material such as calico. This was tried on by the customer and any necessary alterations made before the final garment was cut from the chosen material. Standard patterns from companies such as Butterick had been available since the 1870s. Bespoke clothing is still made this way, whereas most of us buy from a store where there are many different sizes of each style available.

C. F. Winch, milliner, draper and ladies' outfitters, with extensive window displays: Sudbury, c.1905.

Electricity

Framlingham had its first introduction to electric lighting as far back as 1879, when a demonstration was provided one evening in the castle yard. In comparison with gas light the electric light was judged to be very brilliant. The *Framlingham Weekly News* observed that it 'produced a ghastly hue over the countenance, and the shadows cast by objects were very dark'.

Electric lighting systems were being installed in large country houses by Charles Garrard in the late 1890s. These DC (direct current) systems were powered by an engine driven dynamo and batteries. Electric bells were also taking over from mechanical ones. The Crown Hotel had such fittings installed in 1903, with best quality bells

Framlingham's electricity generating plant was located in the old tanyard buildings off Bridge Street. The supply would fail when the meres flooded, which was not an infrequent occurrence, as in this photograph of 1938.

containing platinum contacts, ebony pear push rosettes and Leclanché batteries.

The pioneer of electricity development in Suffolk was Napier Prentice of that prominent Stowmarket family who had various business interests, including the gun cotton factory and fertilisers. On leaving school he was determined to be involved with the development of electricity, and spent some time working in France, where he assisted with patterns for lighting the Paris Opera House. On his return, in conjunction with a business partner, he formed the Suffolk Electricity Supply Co., and started a supply for Stowmarket in 1896. A separate company also manufactured dynamos and motors, with Bull Motors being formed in 1898.

He had earlier written to the managers of many town gas works to try and interest them in providing an electricity supply, as the generating engine could conveniently be powered by gas. There was little interest then, but by 1899 the Ranelagh Gardens in Felixstowe were illuminated by arc lamps, and Diss also had its own supply. In the next few years years other towns followed including Needham Market, Beccles, Braintree and Sudbury. By 1921, residents of Framlingham decided they also needed electricity, as the gas supply was not reliable, with many cuts occurring due to coal shortages.

Discussions were held with the Suffolk Electricity Supply Co., where it was determined that a guarantee of £4,000 would be needed. After a public meeting in the town, A. T. Wicks sent a telegram stating 'Amount guaranteed. Proceed forthwith, letter following'. John Self was appointed chairman of the Advisory Committee, and a bank account opened with Lloyds on the Market Hill.

Premises known as the 'Fellmonger's Yard' (Frank Read's old tannery) were purchased for £450, and deemed suitable as the 'power house'. Approximately 50 people purchased the £1 shares, in amounts varying from £5 to £400. By October 1921, the Electricity Commissioners had provided consent for the supply. Mr Sharratt was appointed district manager for Beccles and Framlingham, with a salary of £225 p.a.

Milton Road, Stowmarket, 1914: gas-powered Fielding & Pratt generator engine being installed in the power station.

Letter from the East Anglian Electric Supply Company in connection with the proposed overhead transmission lines for the new AC supply. Framlingham was the last Suffolk town to be connected to the National Grid, in 1938.

TELEGRAMS: "LECTRIC" STOWMARKET.   TELEPHONE: STOWMARKET 176-9

The East Anglian Electric Supply Company, Limited.

CHIEF OFFICE:- FINBOROUGH HALL, STOWMARKET, SUFFOLK.

ASSOCIATED WITH

FINBOROUGH HALL,
STOWMARKET,
Suffolk.

DIRECTORS.
BRIG.-GEN. WADE H. HAYES (U.S.A.)
F. L. BLAND
THE LORD CRANWORTH, M.C.
COL. C. H. FURNEAUX, D.S.O.
C. H. JONES
A. WINTERBOTTOM
A. ANDERSON, (MANAGING DIRECTOR)

GENERAL MANAGER & ENGINEER
B. G. DRUMMOND, M.I.E.E.

OUR REF.— CBG/GT.

YOUR REF.—

REGISTERED OFFICE:
THAMES HOUSE,
MILLBANK, LONDON, S.W.I.

SUPPLYING ELECTRICITY
IN THE COUNTIES OF
NORFOLK
SUFFOLK
& ESSEX
WITH OFFICES AND
SHOWROOMS AT:-
BECCLES
BRAINTREE
CROMER
DISS
DOWNHAM MARKET
FAKENHAM
FRAMLINGHAM
HADLEIGH
HALESWORTH
HALSTEAD
HARLESTON
HAVERHILL
HOLT
HUNSTANTON
SOUTHWOLD
STOWMARKET
SUDBURY
SHERINGHAM
SWAFFHAM
THETFORD
WITHAM

A.T. Breese, Esq.,
   Grove Hall,
      Ashfield,
         Suffolk.

Dear Sir(s)-or-Madam,

       It is our intention to erect an E.H.T. overhead transmission line between **Debenham......** and **Framlingham.**

       It is proposed that this line should cross your land coloured pink on the enclosed plan. If the route of this line is agreable to you perhaps you would be good enough to sign the enclosed Wayleave Consent Form and return it under cover of the enclosed stamped envelope.

       If you would like to meet our Wayleave Officer and discuss the details we shall be pleased to arrange an appointment accordingly.

       On receipt of the Form completed a copy will be sent to you for your retention.

       Thanking you, I am,

         Yours faithfully,

[signature]

General Manager & Engineer.

Encs:

The company did not have statutory rights, so they were unable to locate poles in the streets. Copper wires were therefore supported from chimneys and poles on private land, with the College being the first place to be connected. Storm damage on one occasion brought the lines down along with the chimney of the College Lodge. The cost of electricity was set at 1*s* 3*d* per unit for lighting.

A 400/200 volt DC three wire system was adopted. Engine breakdowns were often a problem in the early days, and a tractor would be brought in for temporary power. In 1923, a Dorman engine was installed, followed later that year by an ex-marine Campbell 60 hp engine with direct drive to a 30 kw generator, balancing gear and battery.

Water from the old tan yard pits was used to cool the engines. The early diesels had to be started by heating the cylinder heads with a blow torch. Later engines used compressed air, which was a great improvement provided that you had remembered to charge the air bottles the day before.

The installation of Kaleeco wiring systems was carried out by Charles Garrard's company in the 1920s, including the church (eighteen 100-watt, two 200-watt and four 60-watt lamps suspended from wrought iron baskets designed and made in his workshops). In addition, the waiting room, booking hall, signal boxes and goods yard at the station had all been converted from gas to the new source of light.

Financial difficulties within the company were resolved when American investment was obtained, which culminated in 1925 with a change of name to the East Anglian Electricity Supply Company. Cyril Hopes became resident manager at Framlingham the next year, having previously trained with Bull Motors.

Further engines were introduced, including Petter two strokes, but the generating plant was often at risk from bad weather conditions, when flooding of the meres caused the engines to cut out in the rising water. Also, the exposed copper cables would generate impressive blue flashes as they were blown into contact with each other in windy conditions. A similar effect occurred one Gala day, when one of the swing boats on the sale yard ground was caught in the wires causing power failure!

In 1931 Stephen Sullivan joined the company, and would become foreman of the house wiring gangs. The supply was originally only capable of providing power for lighting, but an assisted system was then introduced that allowed three lights and a power plug per house. Improvements came from disposing of the battery and introducing a continuously running generator set with automatic voltage control.

The last engine to be installed was a 50 hp Ruston and Hornsby in 1936, which had a nine-foot diameter flywheel. Its use was short lived though: when the new AC (alternating current) supply from the National Grid became available, the engine ceased operation at 5.45 p.m. on 12th January 1938. Framlingham was the last town in Suffolk to be connected, due to its distance from other major installations. On 1st April 1948, the electricity industry was nationalised.

Gas

The streets of Framlingham were lit by oil lamps from 1832, but when the new gas works commenced operation in 1850, coal gas was used to illuminate 33 second hand street lamps as well as 38 private residences. The gas works were built in College Road at a cost of £1,200, raised by way of £5 shares. Joseph Barker was the first manager, being experienced in such matters, having previously set up a small works to illuminate his premises in Double Street.

He travelled extensively in northern England and Scotland to visit potential suppliers of all the ironwork and fittings required for the works. A contract was placed with Laidlow and Son of Glasgow for £231 13s 0d for the supply of retorts, furnace mountings, stands, bridge pipes, hydraulic main, condenser, purifiers, gas holder, brass syphon pump and much more. The goods were shipped from Newcastle to Snape. Local carter Robert Wright then transported them on to Framlingham, for which he charged seven shillings per ton.

The original works would have been an impressive sight, being constructed from traditional

A partial view of Framlingham gas works, showing the original brick-built structure and chimney of 1850.

materials. There is reference to brickworks at Framlingham, Earl Soham and Brandeston, and Mr Harsant supplied 25,850 bricks at a cost of about £35. A local bricklayer, carpenter and stonemason were employed on the construction.

Gas production started in October 1850, and coal was bought from a Woodbridge merchant at 13 shillings per ton, but cost an extra 6s 6d per ton to be carted to the works. When the railway reached

Framlingham, the coal still had to be laboriously carted from the station, and the initial saving was only about 4%.

The provision of gas for street lighting was established in 1850, but that was only after a public meeting had been held where there was a two-thirds majority in favour, as a charge would need to be made on the rates. Independent local gas inspectors were appointed annually, who contracted with the gas company to supply the gas at an agreed rate. An advertisement was placed in the newspaper, inviting tenders for the supply of gas. Surprising as it may seem, they only received one tender. A meeting was still necessary to decide whether it should be accepted.

The agreement between the Company and the Inspectors specified the annual cost to be paid per lamp (34s 6d in 1900), along with the times they were to be lit, which made allowance for the phase of the moon. The original burners were of the batswing type, which were later replaced by the more efficient incandescent mantle in 1897.

The gas inspectors were not averse to upholding their public duty. They complained that private buyers were getting a more favourable rate for their gas, and the company then offered the inspectors a better rate. The new incandescent lamps gave a much brighter light, as the mantle glowed white

Gas lamps needed regular cleaning, and had to be lit each night. Sudbury, c.1905.

hot, but they were very fragile. There were regular complaints about certain lamps not working, or being turned off early, culminating in a demand for a rebate. In addition to the main street lamps, many shops were lit by gas, along with their own outside lamps.

The following is a very brief description of town gas production. A furnace was used to heat coal in a horizontal retort, which in the absence of air, does not burn. There were eight retorts in the Framlingham works. This process generated the gas along with other by products such as ammonia, hydrogen sulphide and tar. An exhauster pump in conjunction with condensers, washers and purifiers removed these products, and the gas eventually reached the holder. This was a simple

LEFT: *This splendid photograph shows stoker Jack Francis charging one of the horizontal retorts. The vertical pipes take the gas to the hydraulic main. After about four hours, the coke was removed from the retort with long rakes. It was then used to heat the furnace, whose stoke hole is close to the floor in the centre. Manningtree gas works, 1956.*

RIGHT: *Foul lime, cinder, clinker, coke and tar were by-products of gas production, and found a ready market.*

Fo. 580 L .... Oct. 1st 1917

Mr J Breese   Earlstead
Dr. to

The Framlingham Gas Company.
COKE, TAR, BREEZE, &c.
Accounts due every Three Months.
F. G. LING, Secretary.

1917			£	s	d
Feb 8	To 1 Load Foul Lime			1	-
Apl 12	" 1 " " "			1	-
May 19	" 3 " " "			3	-
	" 3 " Cinders			6	-
				11	-

Kindly remit without further delay.

Paid
6th Oct 1917
F.G. Ling

Lavenham gas works. Coke was a by-product of the coal gas process and used for heating the retorts. Any excess was sold to the public. The weighing scales are just visible next to the coke pile. The vertical pipes are the condenser, where the gas was cooled.

but most effective arrangement which can be considered as an open ended drum with water in it. Another smaller inverted drum is located inside. When gas is pumped in, the inner drum rises, with the water maintaining the seal. The weight of the drum provided the pressure to distribute the gas throughout the town.

The condensed tar found a ready market for various sealing and waterproofing purposes, while the coke formed in the retorts was then used in the furnaces, with the excess being sold. To see a preserved non-working town gas works, visit the Fakenham Gas Museum in Norfolk.

By the turn of the century most businesses in the town and many houses had the benefit of gas lighting. Charles Garrard was manager of the gas works, and his business derived much revenue from work on these installations.

In 1908, the Framlingham Gas Light and Coke Company was paying a dividend of 6%. That year, 400 tons of coal were carbonised, producing 3.8 million cubic feet of gas, at a sale price of five shillings per cubic foot. There were 140 consumers, along with 55 street lights. Gas was also being promoted for uses apart from lighting. An exhibition held in the Foresters' Hall in 1908 displayed a large number of cookers, radiators, kettles, heaters and fires.

In 1949, the undertaking became part of the Ipswich Division of the Eastern Gas Board, but much of the original brick structure had been replaced by then with corrugated sheets, along with a steel chimney. It was a real eyesore, but that is all gone now. Large butane gas cylinders were introduced from 1953, and 20 years later North Sea gas was directly piped to the town. The College Road site is now desolate.

Towards the end of its working life, a tall steel chimney had replaced the brick one. The building had been modified over many years and became a most unattractive part of the townscape. The last gas powered street light is visible in this photograph.

The Grocer

The grocery trade was well established on the Market Hill by the beginning of the twentieth century, although in earlier years it was often combined with that of the draper. George and Charles Edwards developed their business in the 1820s and supplied goods to shops as far afield as Halesworth and Aldeburgh. They dissolved their partnership when George went into malting and farming, while Charles continued to run the grocery business which eventually passed to Jonathan Hart and then Samuel Green Carley. Samuel was born in Badingham and became an apprentice grocer in Laxfield. He gained further experience in London and elsewhere before settling in Framlingham, where he traded as grocer and Italian Warehouseman, dealing in Italian groceries, fruits, olive oil etc.

By 1900, Samuel and his brother Robert were running one of the foremost grocery businesses in the county. There was plenty of competition, though, with Charles Cooke on the corner of Crown and Anchor Lane, Jude on the opposite side of Market Hill, and Dorling in Bridge Street.

In 1910, a branch of the International (Tea Company's) Stores opened in Bridge Street, but Carleys remained the established Framlingham grocers and wine merchants, providing a personal service to their customers.

The grocer (from gross = 12 dozen) bought his goods in bulk, which would then be weighed out to suit the customer's requirements and put into bags folded from flat sheet. Sugar, for example, would arrive in hundredweight sacks at the station. Bob Scoggins, the GER delivery man, would then cart

Competition for Framlingham grocers arrived in 1910, when the International Stores opened their shop in Bridge Street. They soon became established throughout Suffolk.

them to the store room. Prior to that, sugar came in loaves which were then reduced in size by the grocer. If the sugar were to be sifted, it would first of all need to be ground with pestle and mortar. The wooden wall crane used for unloading and taking goods into the upper floor has been rebuilt in recent times by Tony Martin, and can be seen to the rear of the property. Teas were delivered in

Most goods arrived at Carley's in bulk and had to be raised to the first floor store room. Their crane for that purpose was photographed around 1975 and a reproduction still exists.

large chests, before blending and packing to the customer's own requirements, costing about 1*s* 6*d* per lb. Salt blocks could be obtained from the salt works in Southwold until the late 1800s. All these goods, along with soap, tobacco, dried fruits and coffee etc., would need considerable manhandling, cleaning, weighing and packaging before they were ready for the customer. Carley's shop, along with others in the town, would stay open well into the evening to complete orders.

Customers, depending on their status, would leave their shopping list, which would be made up and delivered, with the goods going on account. Several products which are still well known to us were available, e.g. Bovril, Hartley's jam, Brooke Bond tea, Lea and Perrins' sauce, Robertson's marmalade and Patum Peperium (a pâté made from anchovy, butter, herbs and spice, and popularly sold as 'Gentleman's Relish').

Account customers were provided with a hard backed book, with gold embossed lettering, 'S. G. Carley & Co., Family Grocers, Framlingham'. James Breese's account book for 1897 shows that the bill was only settled once a year, at the end of December. For that year, the sum was £17 3*s* 2*d*, but that was offset by the substantial amount of £9 13*s* 7*d* for credits. These mainly related to the supply of large quantities of eggs, along with some chickens and turkeys from his farm.

Wright's family grocer, Market Hill, Sudbury, c.1905. These premises and those of Carley and Webb in Framlingham provided a specialist grocery service for over 100 years, but the former closed at the end of 2006.

Carley's account for 1903.

Typical purchases in 1897 were:

tin coffee	9*d*
bloater paste	2½*d*
½ *lb.* tea	11*d*
tin salmon	9*d*
4 *lb.* sugar	10*d*
tin lobster	1*s* 1*d*
½ *lb.* cayenne pepper	1*s* 0*d*
Lifebuoy soap	3*d*
½ *lb.* tobacco	2*s* 0*d*
Blue starch	5*d*
60 cartridges	4*s* 0*d*
1 gal Crystal oil	10*d*

Carley's services included wines and spirits. They were agents for W. & A. Gilbey's, and stocked Guinness and various bitters at a shilling per gallon, in 9 or 18 gallon casks. It was Edward Lankester who specialised in this sector from his adjacent premises in Crown and Anchor Lane. Walter Cocks continued the business until his death in 1922, when Carleys acquired it.

The candle trade had always been considerable, and many grocers made their own. Joseph Baxter took over the Edwards business in candles, but by the turn of the century candle making had died out in the town, as gas and oil lighting were in common use.

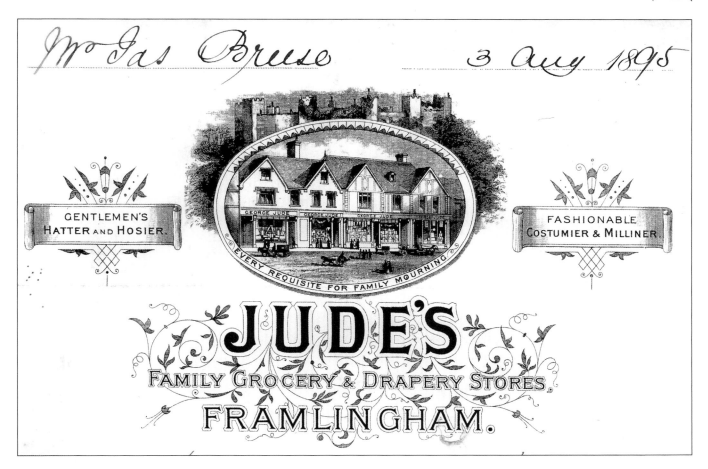

Mr Jas Bruce   *3 Aug 1895*

GENTLEMEN'S
HATTER and HOSIER.

FASHIONABLE
COSTUMIER & MILLINER.

GEORGE JUDE   GEORGE JUDE   GEORGE JUDE

EVERY REQUISITE FOR FAMILY MOURNING

JUDE'S
FAMILY GROCERY & DRAPERY STORES,
FRAMLINGHAM.

George Jude combined the business of grocer and draper at his large Market Hill establishment.
Twelve assistants lived in the house, in addition to his family and domestic staff.

The Gunsmith

Shooting was an important activity for farmers, and it was essential to have a local shop that could provide all the necessary ammunition, along with the repair and sale of guns. Benjamin Norman had served an apprenticeship with James Purdey, the renowned London gunsmith, prior to opening his Church Street shop in 1870, where he manufactured a wide range of guns. Most other sporting goods were also catered for, including tennis, cricket and football. Normans were also well known for their own particular type of low bias wooden bowling wood which was known as a 'Fram'.

Norman's gun shop in Church Street, with three generations of the family. Ben, on the right, was trained at Purdey's in London, before opening this shop in 1870. His son William is to the left, with grandson Ben in the centre.

DAN SCASE,
GUN, AMMUNITION AND CYCLE DEPOT,
Market Hall, FRAMLINGHAM.

Why Pay your so-called Gun-Makers

50 to 55 % on Guns, and 20 to 25 % on Cartridges,

When you can save this
By dealing with the Manufacturers' Agent.

£6 10s.   £6 10s.

First-class Double-barrelled Hammerless Guns
ANSEN AND DULEY SYSTEM.

A most superior Gun.   Handsomely engraved.   Finely Figured.   Walnut Stock. The Barrels are of Best Quality Special Steel or Extra Quality English Damascus. These are Treble-wedge Fast Action, truly Circular-jointed, and with Automatic Safety Bolt.

Gun with Hammers (same quality as Hammerless) **£5 10s.**

My Gun for Farmer's or Gamekeeper's use	4	0	0
My Strong Gun for Rough Work	3	10	0
Ditto	2	10	0

Single-barrel Breech-loading Guns, 13/6, 15/6, 18/6, & 20/-
Rook, Rabbit, and Saloon Rifles from 10/-
N.B.—Every Gun is shot by D.S. in the open, and my £3 10s. 0d. is capable of making a Pattern of at least 200 shots in a 30-inch circle at 40 yards.

Call and see one tested.

My Sudden Death, Green Cases, loaded with 3 ds. Black Powder, 1¼ shot, 6/6 per 100
My Perfection Cartridge, loaded with Smokeless Powder   ...   8/-   ,,
My Perfection Cartridge, loaded with E S, S S, Kynoch or Schultze   9/-   ,,
My Demon Brand, Smokeless Cartridge   10/- per 100.   Chilled Shot 10/6   ,,
I should like it to be clearly understood that no better Cartridge than my Demon Brand can be bought at any price. Greatest possible care is exercised in the loading and turning over of the ends, and I have great confidence in offering them as equal to any Cartridge in the Market
Special Cartridges for Pigeon and Wild Fowl Shooting in Stock.

SCASE's Cycles still to the Front ; this has been achieved without the publication of Testimonials

Look out for my 1901 Monarchs, Gent's, £7 10s., Lady's £7 10s.
All my Machines and Tyres are guaranteed for 12 months

Dan Scase was an expert shot, and competed at Bisley. His Market Hill shop sold a wide range of stock, including guns, sports goods and bicycles.

Competition was not far away though, as Dan Scase opened a general store on the Market Hill, which also sold guns, rifles, air guns, revolvers, cartridges and sporting equipment. Dan was an expert shot and represented the Framlingham Volunteers at Bisley. The Challenge hammerless double barrel shot gun was available for £7, while his cheapest cartridges, sold under the name 'Sudden Death', were 6s 6d per 100. His advertisements were challenging – 'why pay your so-called gun makers 50 to 55% on guns, when you can save this by dealing with the manufacturer's agent?' Was this a direct dig at Norman's?

The description of gunmaker needs some clarification. In practice, this usually meant buying in the main components (barrel, firing mechanism and stock). These would be assembled and personalised to the owner, and inscribed with the 'maker's' name. The local gunsmith would certainly be proficient in making parts to repair a gun, or manufacturing a new stock.

Ammunition would also be made on the premises, with the percussion caps, cases and powder being bought in and assembled. The maker's name could be printed on the cases when purchased from his supplier.

Hunting and shooting were the backbone of social life for farmers and landowners, while many would use a gun to augment food for the table. Normans

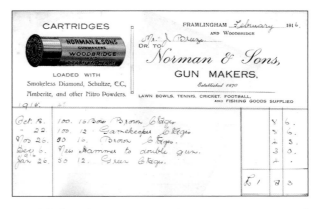

1916 bill for cartridges, and fitting a new hammer to a double-barrelled gun.

provided an important service to gun owners and sporting enthusiasts up until its closure in 1960. It was also a fascinating shop for boys, where they could buy catapult elastic and fishing tackle, surrounded by displays of guns and cartridges.

Shooting was popular as a sport, and a successful day would bring a welcome addition to the table. How many people today would be prepared to skin and clean rabbits for cooking?

The Ironmonger

The ironmonger needed to hold an extensive range of goods to cover the needs of local tradesmen, farmers and householders. Since the early nineteenth century the Black Country in the West Midlands had been producing large quantities of nails, screws, nuts, bolts, hinges etc., which could later be transported by rail throughout the country.

William Barker had an established ironmongery shop just off the Market Hill, employing three men and two boys, as well as another shop in Aldeburgh. His stock book of 1893 is illustrated by many sketches, and provides a fascinating insight to the size of his business. The premises consisted of the pail room, glass room, stove room, bolt and nut room, various warehouses, coach house, scythe stone room (over 1,200 in stock), nail and oil room, sheet iron warehouse, iron warehouse, bar iron warehouse, workshop and sale shop. The contents of the workshop show they were able to offer a wide range of services, e.g. large range of hand tools, soldering irons, pipe cutters, vices, anvil and bellows, drilling machine, lawn mower knife grinder with belts and shafting, lathe, pipe screwing machine, punching machine, tyre bender and much more. Communication between the workshop and office was by a speaking tube consisting of 120 feet of gas pipe with two mouth pieces and whistles. The black mare, two-wheel dog cart and two business carts were valued at £40.

The goods in the shop were marked with a code to show cost and retail prices, to allow some degree of manoeuvring when a purchaser wanted to

William Barker sold his established ironmongery business to Charles Garrard in 1897. This account is for engine packing and cotton waste.

haggle over the price. Barker's simple code was as follows:

1	2	3	4	5	6	7	8	9	10
S	M	A	L	P	R	O	F	I	T

Competition from other outlets would suggest that SMALL PROFIT was most appropriate.

In addition to the usual range of ironmongery and tools, domestic goods were also stocked, typical examples from 1897 being listed overleaf.

A wide range of glass lamps were kept by William Barker. From his stock-taking book of 1893.

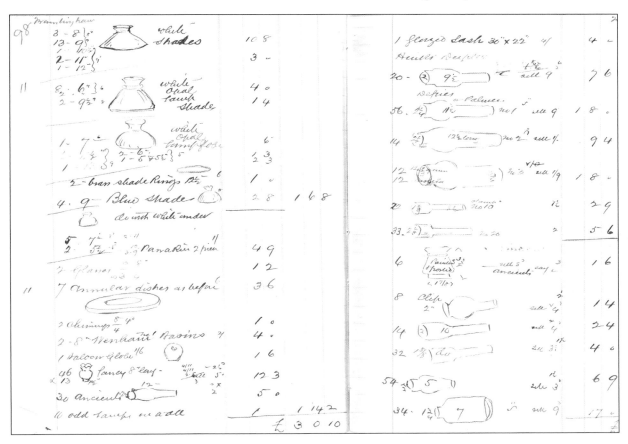

Mr J. Breese, Church Farm, Saxstead

FURNISHING AND GENERAL IRONMONGERY WAREHOUSE,
Market Place, FRAMLINGHAM, Suffolk,
AND EASTON.

30 June 1910

J. N. Breese

Bought of CHARLES GARRARD,

BAR IRON, OIL & COLOUR MERCHANT,

HOT WATER, SANITARY, GAS AND ELECTRICAL ENGINEER.

ESTIMATES FREE. MOTOR ENGINEER. WORKMEN FOR REPAIRS.

A Large Stock OF STOVES AND RANGES

Telephone :—No. 7.
Telegrams :—Garrard, Framlingham.

ALL ACCOUNTS RENDERED QUARTERLY.

1910							
May 9	1 Jack Plane	4/6	1 Smooth Plane	4/3	10	9
	1 Hand Saw	3/9	1 Tenon Saw	3/3	7	0
	1 Pad Saw + Blade				1	6
	1 Spokeshave	8	1 Turnscrew ea 6 + 9		1	11
	1 Tower Pincers	1/-	1 Rule	1/=	2	0
	1 Gilstons	2/-		1/6	3	6
	1 Firmer Chisel each 3/8				1	6
	1 Hammer 1/- 2 Gimlets 3				1	10

CHARLES GARRARD
PAID
16 JUL 1910
WITH THANKS
FRAMLINGHAM

With Compliments.

£1 . 10 . 0

Account from 1910 for various carpenters' tools.

Robert Autey's ironmongery shop in Bridge Street c. 1890. The hay knife fixed to the wall, to the left of the drainpipe, was used to cut the compacted hay from the stack.

ASPINALL'S ENAMEL.

ASPINALL'S ENAMEL

COLOURS— EXQUISITE.
SURFACE— LIKE PORCELAIN.

No 24 1890

Breese

Bought of

R. H. AUTEY,
Tool, Cutlery, and Ironmongery Stores,
Bridge Street,
Framlingham.

1/2 dz Saw Files 0 8d	4	0

Paid
R H Autey

Robert Autey bill of 1890 for saw files.

enamelled saucepans	1s 2d -- 3s	4d
patent safety razor	5s	0d
bird cage	1s	10d
iron bedsteads	9s 9d – 13s	9d
gravy strainer	1s	0d
perambulator	19s	0d
brass bedwarmer	1s	6d
coffee pots	4½d – 2s	10d
E.P. cake knife & fork	12s	6d
goffering iron		8d

Electro plated (EP) metal goods were popular.

Barker's large ironmongery business was taken over by Charles Garrard in 1897. He expanded further into general household goods, as well as bicycles and the town's first motor garage. This was now the age of mass production of most of the ironmonger's stock, and travelling salesmen would call regularly to promote their products.

The core of the ironmonger's daily routine changed little, with much heavy lifting and long hours. Nails for example, were supplied in large

sacks, which had to be transferred to the bins in the shop. These were weighed on the counter scales for the customer's order, and then wrapped in brown paper. Every conceivable part of the shop and storerooms was used and the ceiling was an

Garrard's ironmongery shop, c. 1910. From the left, Stanley Capon, Charles Garrard, Bernard Roe and Bob Moore. Note the fine gas lamp to illuminate the outside of his premises. He was also manager of the gas works, and his company installed pipework and fittings for the consumers.

CHARLES GARRARD, MARKET PLACE, FRAMLINGHAM. SUFFOLK.

Ironmonger and Engineer.

Telephone No. 7

Telegrams—
"Garrard, Framlingham."

area not to be missed, being hung with kettles, lamps, pots, mole traps and much more.

Along with most shops, the opening hours were long, and on Saturdays could be up to 8 or 9 p.m. if there were still customers. The Shops Act of 1912 introduced closing at 1 p.m. on Wednesdays, which was still a common practice in the latter part of the twentieth century.

In an age when nothing of value was thrown away, the ironmonger's workshop would repair or even remake the various broken household items, a typical example from 1902 being: 'making new heavy wrought iron bottom grate for range, and sending man to measure for same – 5/9.'

The farm worker used a number of hand tools, and replacement handles were kept in stock for them. A new spade handle, for example, would be shaped to size with a drawknife, and then riveted into place; all part of the service. Saw sharpening would also be taken in, but often passed on to another tradesman who specialised in the setting and sharpening.

There were other smaller ironmongers in the town, such as Robert Autey in Bridge Street, while Jarvis Scoggins' general store in Well Close Square could provide most household requirements. Fruer Bridges' blacksmith and ironmongery business was of a similar size to Garrard's, but in those days the emphasis was more on the agricultural side rather than domestic. A new glass fronted shop was built next to the Fore Street forge in 1907, which provided better facilities for the display of garden implements and ironmongery. In 1961, the business of Charles Garrard was bought by A.E. Bridges Ltd., to become Bridges and Garrards Ltd., maintaining a link to the first Silvanus Bridges who set up as a blacksmith in Double Street, around 1724.

IRONMONGER PORTWAY and Co HOT WATER AND SANITARY ENGINEERS

Hot & Cold Water, & Gas Engineers.

Telephone and Electric Bell Fitters.

PORTWAY & Co., 32, KING ST., SUDBURY.

EXPERTS on HEATING, VENTILATING, and SANITARY PLUMBING, WELL WORK and PUMPING APPLIANCES, BATHS, DOMESTIC WATER SUPPLY, AND DRAINAGE.

GARDEN AND GREENHOUSE REQUISITES.

OUTDOOR GAMES.

AMMUNITION.   GUNS.

Furnishing Ironmongers & Cutlers.

ESTIMATES & REPORTS CAREFULLY PREPARED.

Portway and Co. of Sudbury offered a wide range of services in addition to that of ironmonger. Note the sign for 'Oil and Colourmen' over the doorway. The same wording can still be seen above the ironmonger's shop in Clare.

The Maltster

Malt is the prime ingredient of beer, and is made through the process of malting barley grain. This began with the barley being steeped in water to start the germination process, whereby the starch changes to malt sugar. It was then transferred to the malt floor using the wooden shovels and spread to a depth that varied between about three and eighteen inches. The greater depth was necessary in winter to build up the temperature, with the opposite requirement in warmer weather. This had to be turned and aerated two or three times a day to prevent the germinating roots forming an entangled mat, and to allow heat to escape.

This illustration from James Maulden's account of 1897 shows the maltings to the left, with vapour leaving the roof vent of the kiln.

When germination had reached the stage which the foreman maltster judged right, the 'green' malt was moved to the kiln, which had a floor of ventilated tiles with the furnace below. The heat evaporated the water, producing the characteristic condensing vapour from the roof vents. This drying process stops the germination while higher temperatures provide more flavour and colour. Following screening to remove the rootlets, the malted barley was bagged for despatch to the brewery. Before the brewer can use the malt, it has to be crushed to expose the endosperm. James Maulden had a horse driven mill for this purpose, although large brewers would have their own. Malting was mainly limited to the colder months. Changes to the temperature of the malting floor could only be made by adjustment to the cross flow of air through windows by opening or closing wooden shutters. The process could last from about five to 12 days, being longest in the cold weather. Malting ceased in summer as warm weather could promote the growth of harmful moulds in the malt.

The large brewer, as well as the home brewer, all required malt, and there have been at least five maltings in Framlingham. The largest of these was built for George Brooke Keer on premises which extended along Crown & Anchor Lane and into Fore Street, with the present Garrards Court being the main malt house. These extensive facilities included a brewery which served the 21 pubs that he owned in the town and surrounding area, but his spectacular bankruptcy in 1832 resulted in all these properties being auctioned.

The last maltster in Framlingham was Edwin Clarke, who initially operated from Brooke Keer's old premises in Fore Street, and then the Haynings maltings in Castle Street, previously occupied by George Edwards. In 1879 James Maulden purchased the Bridge Street maltings, which consisted of a steep, malt floor, kiln and horse driven malt mill.

This extensive range of maltings was located on the Gipping at Stowmarket. By the time of this photo, c.1920, the malt was transported by rail, whereas in an earlier time, the navigation had been important.

When James died in 1905, the malt side of his business contained a 25 coomb steep, two barley chambers capable of holding 1,500 coomb, warehousing for 700 coomb, along with loading floor and hop house. There were three wells on the site, claimed to provide an unlimited supply of water.

The demise of the rural beer houses and Framlingham's brewery would have reduced the local demand for malt. The breweries in the large towns often had maltings close to them, which could supply their demands at a better price. Geoffrey Clarke, a grandson of Edwin, came into the business in 1933 and recalled working in the Haynings malting. By this time malt production was in a very small way, and had ceased by

Malt kiln vent from George Brooke Keer's original premises to the rear of Garrard's Court in Fore Street, photographed in the 1970s.

Edwin Clarke started business in Framlingham as a malt-ster. This account covers a wide range of goods including cotton cake, coal, peas, maize, malt and hops.

around 1937, although the company continued to pay a nominal £1 membership to the Maltsters Association until 1947. The steep was located outside the building, with the coal fired furnace below ground level of the main wooden structure. Many farmers and individuals would brew their own beer, and buy malt by the bushel, but this demand fell in the early twentieth century, and finally ended the need for small scale malt production.

Many farm workers were laid off after the harvest and the malting trade might enable them to gain further employment if they were prepared to travel. Even a horseman with more assured work might leave the land, with the prospect of tripling his wages to about 38 shillings per week.

The large breweries in Burton on Trent had their own maltings and needed many workers for the

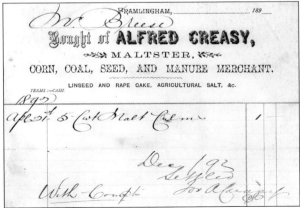

Alfred Creasy's bill for 5 cwt of malt culms. These were the dried rootlets of the malted barley, which were used by farmers as animal feed.

winter period. Norfolk and Suffolk were the main areas for this migration, and the men were referred to as 'Norkies'. Agents interviewed the men at several locations, including the Crown Hotel in Framlingham. Provided they were well built (and supposedly over 21 in the later period), an agreement would be signed and they would be provided with a single rail ticket to Burton on Trent. Many left from Framlingham station in mid-September, returning at the end of the malting season in May ready for the hay harvest (haysel). This exodus occurred between about 1870 and 1930. In 1904, 169 Suffolk men were employed in one Burton maltings alone. The work was extremely hard prior to mechanisation, when the coomb sacks (weighing about 16 stones) had to be carried up stairs and along the floors within the maltings buildings, often over a distance of at least 100 yards each time.

The temperatures on the kiln floor were unbearable, often in excess of $210°$F towards the end of the process, and claims of drinking sixteen pints of beer afterwards, with no effect, were common. The work went on for seven days a week, every week of the season, and what with the various fights that broke out between the mixed workforce, one needed to be of considerable strength and stamina to survive. The Bygones video *Gone To Burton*, produced by Anglia TV, vividly shows a recreation of the old malting process, with two of the original workers telling their story in the Crown Hotel, Framlingham in 1974.

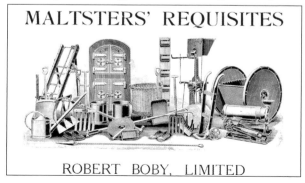

MALTSTERS' REQUISITES

ROBERT BOBY, LIMITED

The Miller

The power of wind and water had been used for centuries to turn the millstones which ground the corn. In an industrial age though, it was not practical or economical to rely on nature, and few windmills were built beyond the 1860s, when steam power was increasingly being used to drive the mill stones. The first purpose built steam milling premises in Framlingham were constructed in 1853, but the venture was short lived due to insufficient capacity in the machinery and stones, which had been purchased second hand. The building fortunately survived and is now the United Free Church in Albert Place.

The application of steam power to existing windmills was an obvious development as the miller could then determine when he worked, not being at the mercy of the elements. Steam was first used in Frederick Kindred's tower mill in Victoria Mill Road, which had been built in 1843 for his brother John, by John Whitmore of Wickham Market. He subsequently sold it to Thomas Buckmaster, who built a complete steam mill on the same site, which was later operated by his son John. The tower mill was noted as being derelict in 1926, and was demolished in 1935.

Benefiting from a raised location, there had been a long established windmill at Mount Pleasant and at times there were two mills. Reuben Whitehead had operated the post mill for many years before erecting a steam mill on that site around 1880. The business then passed to Augustus Roe, who later started the East Anglian Bacon Curing Co. Ltd. at Broadwater. The whole venture went into liquidation in 1900, after which Frederick Button bought the Mount Pleasant post mill and premises for £550. He had previously set up a steam mill with a pair of French stones on the site of an earlier tannery and smock mill in Station Road. In the early twentieth century steam power was often replaced by oil engines, but prior to that there had been four separate steam powered mills in the town.

Frederick Button had been a tenant of the Mount Pleasant mill before Reuben Whitehead sold it in 1887. He then set up a steam mill in Station Road, near the old smock mill, but in 1900 was able to buy the Mount Pleasant mill following the bankruptcy of Augustus Roe.

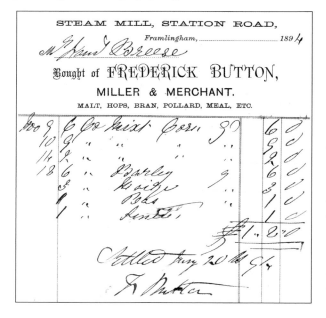

The milling process itself consisted of a stationary circular bedstone and the upper running stone which revolved in close proximity to it. The upper stone was driven from above in an overdrift mill, and from below in an underdrift mill. Corn was fed into the centre of the stone, and ground between the surfaces before emerging as meal at the perimeter. The French burr stones were best for producing fine flour, but were expensive as they were made up from several sections, and also had to be imported. Derbyshire stones were in one

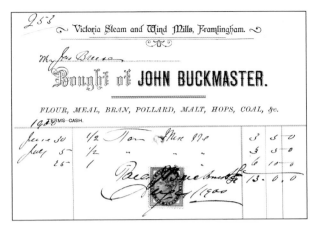

Wind and steam power were both in use at the turn of the century, but the sails of the mill were removed around 1918, and the tower demolished in 1935.

piece, but wore quicker and were more suitable for animal feed production. All types would need dressing as the surfaces wore down.

The 1901 census shows two men in the town with the occupation of millstone dresser. They used a mill 'bill', which consisted of a turned wooden mallet (thrift) with a special steel insert, to re-cut the grooves in the stones. The 'bill' was chisel shaped, while a 'pick' was pointed. The process associated with sharpening the tool was another of the mysterious powers of the blacksmith.

The miller had to be experienced in setting up the machinery, and reading the weather; if he failed to

BELOW: *The introduction of the more efficient roller mill process in 1891 by James Maulden affected the commercial viability of the other local mills. This 1896 account shows various items purchased, which have been offset by 80 coombs of wheat. The illustration, with considerable artistic licence, was produced by the company that he purchased in the same year.*

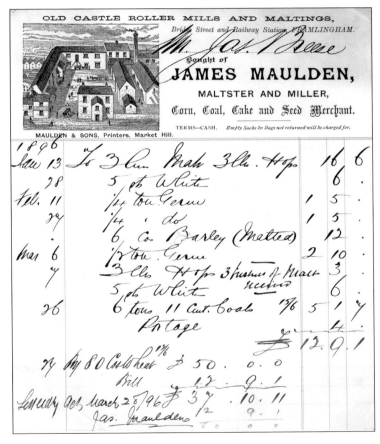

do so, changing conditions could lead to disaster. In earlier times he was a fairly wealthy person, with his recompense for grinding the corn usually being a percentage of the flour produced.

Flour milling by the traditional millstone method was becoming uneconomical by the late nineteenth century. Many windmills went over to animal feed production, but eventually the need for a single costly repair would herald the end of the mill's working life. In 1926, Rex Wailes' survey of Suffolk windmills showed that there were 58 windmills still working, which had slumped to 13 by 1939. In addition, there were six power driven windmills. Many became idle as their work was consumed by the more efficient roller mills, often built in the large towns and ports. Cranfields opened their Ipswich roller mill in 1884. Framlingham was not to be left behind in

this respect. James Maulden had purchased the old maltings in Bridge Street for £600 in 1879, which became a thriving business with malting along with the introduction around 1884 of milling by two pairs of four-foot diameter French burr grist stones driven by a portable steam engine. Coal, coke, tea, tobacco and cigars also became part of his trade, but it was the installation in 1891 of a complete roller mill by Whitmore and Binyon that transformed the business.

George Binyon went into partnership with William Whitmore in 1868, which precipitated the expansion of the Wickham Market company. They manufactured many products including sluice gates, wind and steam powered milling equipment, and later the rolling mill machinery, which was exported to many countries. This was a rare example of a large engineering works in a small town, but it barely survived into the twentieth century.

Two boilers were used to raise the steam for the 40 hp compound engine, with its high and low pressure cylinders and a condenser. The roller process differs from conventional millstone grinding in that the corn is passed through a series of rollers, which rotate at different speeds. The flour is thus produced through various stages of reduction, which are followed by different separations.

The plant could produce 20 sacks of flour per day,

Part of original conveyor system from Maulden's Whitmore and Binyon roller mill.

and at one time the firm was the largest employer in Framlingham. A sack of flour weighed 20 stone. Every morning, yellow painted tumbrels and wagons pulled by Suffolk horses could be seen leaving Bridge Street, loaded with sacks of flour. By 1898

Victoria roller mill, Swilland, c.1926. The photograph captures the full range of transport in use at that time: horse and wagon, Model T Fords and a 1913 Foden 3-ton steam wagon. The mill belonged to Colonel C. A. Barron, who is seated immediately to the left of the Model T. You could telephone an order to him on Witnesham 4.

Maulden had 40 agents for his products in all the surrounding towns and villages.

These premises were extensive, and in addition to the milling and malting facilities, there were horse stables, van sheds, a harness room, offices, plus oil and coke stores. Maulden also owned granaries and stores along Station Road, but these were sold after James died in 1905. Two of his sons, James and William, continued the business, but James later moved to run their mill at Kelsale. William was joined by his sons, Willoughby and Stanley, who operated the mill up to 1946. The combined effects of commercial pressures, limited site access and reliance on steam power saw flour milling cease then, although they continued to trade in other areas, such as coal and animal feed, until the site was sold in 1955. A Whitmore and Binyon roller mill can be seen at the Alton Mill, the Museum of East Anglian Life, Stowmarket.

Whitmore and Binyon of Wickham Market expanded their engineering works from the 1870s. They went on to manufacture complete roller mill installations which were exported to many countries, but financial difficulties forced closure in 1901.

William Maulden at the entrance to his roller mill works in Bridge Street.

WHITMORE & BINYON

Millwrights, Engineers, Founders & Boiler Makers,

Iron Works: WICKHAM MARKET, SUFFOLK,

And 28, MARK LANE, LONDON, E.C.

Telegraphic Addresses: "ACCELERATE, LONDON." "WORKS, WICKHAM MARKET."

MILLING ON THE NEW SYSTEMS.

Millers contemplating the conversion of Stone to Roller Plants or the putting up of Complete Mills on the Gradual Reduction System by Rolls, are respectfully invited to communicate with WHITMORE & BINYON whose recently increased plant and conveniences will enable them to execute orders with despatch.

NEWLY IMPROVED FOUR-ROLLER MILL,

For Wheat Breaks or Middlings Reduction, with Lever Apparatus for simultaneously spreading the Rolls and arresting the feed.

BRAN CLEANING ROLLS of Superior Make. Made with or without countershafts.

The Motor and Cycle Agent

The motor agent did not suddenly start in business when the first car appeared. It was to be a process of evolution, often from the cycle dealers who became established in late Victorian times. Their knowledge of wheels, gears, chains, sprockets etc. would set them in good stead for the car or motorcycle, although the internal combustion engine itself was something of a mystery in the early days.

Suffolk had its fair share of car and motorcycle manufacturers before the First World War, with production mainly centred in Beccles, Lowestoft, Stowmarket and Woodbridge. J. W. Brooke and Co. of Lowestoft were most prolific, with their first three cylinder car being designed in 1900. This was followed by a four cylinder model, and then a more powerful 40hp six cylinder model in 1906. Their extensive marine engineering works allowed them to manufacture their own engines, whereas other local suppliers relied on proprietary engines. Competition was always strong in the motor industry, and Brooke ceased development to concentrate on the marine side, although their cars were still available until around 1913.

Cars were manufactured in some Suffolk towns.
J. W. Brooke and Co. of Lowestoft designed and manufactured a range of quality cars between 1900 and 1913.
This photograph is of a four-cylinder 1904 model with landaulette body. 1906 saw the introduction of their six-cylinder engine, with a cost of approximately £685 for the bare chassis unit, and £850 for the limousine.

Arthur Potter, with his son Horry, exhibiting bicycles at the horse show, c.1907.

Charles Garrard was an agent for Gladiator and Napier before adding Ford and Argyll around 1907–08. This page is from the 1911 catalogue: the Model T roadster and open runabout cost £170.

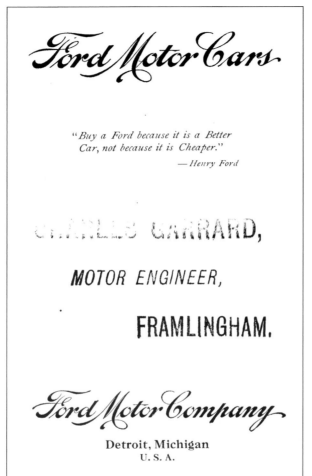

Ford Motor Cars

"Buy a Ford because it is a Better Car, not because it is Cheaper."
— Henry Ford

CHARLES GARRARD,
MOTOR ENGINEER,
FRAMLINGHAM.

Ford Motor Company
Detroit, Michigan
U. S. A.

Charles Garrard opened the first garage in Framlingham around 1900 in the old Fore Street maltings, being some four years after the law changed to allow light motor vehicles on the road at speeds up to 12 mph. His large ironmongery business provided the background which allowed him to deal in new cars, and by 1905 he held agencies for Napier and Gladiator, to be followed by Ford and Argyll in 1907–8. Charles Garrard was the first Ford agent in the town, before the introduction of the legendary Model T. In this period, petrol was delivered in sealed two gallon cans on a horse and wagon, from the Anglo American Oil Company depot at Campsea Ash. It was sold under the trade name of Pratts, and cost two shillings a gallon. Around 1925, that company opened

Petrol was originally delivered to Framlingham in two-gallon cans, by horse and wagon. The Anglo-American Oil Company opened a depot in Station Road around 1925, where oil and petrol were stored in large tanks.

| L.P.S. | Form 2051. | INVOICE. No. A 814141 |

a depot in Station Road, where two large silver painted tanks contained White Rose and Royal Daylight oil for lamps and heating, along with a third one for petroleum.

A. G. Potter had served his apprenticeship as a blacksmith in Needham Market, and raced 'penny farthing' bicycles before moving to Framlingham and setting up in trade as an osier merchant (osiers are the shoots of the willow tree) and basket maker in Station Road. He then moved into bicycle sales and repair, with popular makes such as Swift and Raleigh. These arrived three to a crate at the station, and would be assembled in the cycle shop

Potter's business evolved from baskets through bicycles and onto cars and tractors. This AC Sociable with tiller steering was used as an early runabout. Rear left, Gee Williams, Morgan Watts, A. G. Potter, his wife Rose, and Shumpty Thorpe. Their children, from the left, Horry, Phyllis, Don and Jack, c.1910.

and old Reading Room in Brook Lane, by Morgan Watts, his first employee. His own make of bicycle was also sold, called the 'Fram'.

The trade in those times was very reliant on the skills of the workmen to repair or fabricate parts to keep a bicycle or car on the road. Tyres were expensive, and would be subject to many gashes due to the poor road conditions. Gaiters were made up to extend the tyre life. Morgan even made an accumulator to charge batteries by the use of zinc rods, porous pots and sulphuric acid. In 1912, Robert Hawes was apprenticed to learn the business of cycle and motor agent. His Articles of Agreement stated that in return for a payment of £20 from Hawes, A. G. Potter would take him into employment for six months and pay him a salary of 10 shillings a week.

Potter became a sub-dealer for Ford under Charles Garrard in 1913. This bill of the same year is for the hire of his land-aulette, which is the style of bodywork in the illustration.

The big change for Potter came in 1913, when he was offered a Ford sub dealership under Charles Garrard, and was committed to selling three cars in that first year, increasing to 25 in 1915. He was limited to selling the cars in the town and within a two mile radius of the station. A £30 deposit was required, which was forfeited if he did not buy the agreed number of cars for that year. By 1920 Potter proudly claimed that he was the authorised Ford dealer. Garrard then concentrated on Overland and Morris cars.

There was to be more competition after the First World War. In 1922, Leonard Walne set up his garage in Riverside, and certainly had experience of the motor trade, having worked for Rolls Royce,

Drink-driving accident 1909. A. G. Potter (hands on hips) forlornly inspects the damage to his Vulcan hire car. Shumpty Thorpe was driving the car down Fore Street. On turning into Station Road, he was confronted by a horse and trap on the wrong side of the road, with drunken farmer on board. The building in the distance was originally a steam mill, and survives as the United Free Church.

Armstrong Siddeley, Lock and Stagg, Egertons and the Lindsey Motor Company, who had manufactured cars in Woodbridge. Potter's business expanded with the initial popularity of the Model T, but in the post war period this car was becoming outdated, and sales fell. It was also penalised by the 20 hp rating of its 2.9 litre engine, as a new tax introduced in 1920 levied a charge of £1 per hp. The Fordson tractor side was important to him, particularly when there were long delays in receiving the new Model A car, and in the subsequent depression of the early 1930s. An agreement had been signed with Mann Egerton of Norwich to become a sub dealer for Fordson tractors in 1918.

Other business also showed the same development pattern from bicycles through to cars. Arthur Shulver had his Castle Cycle and Motor Works in Well Close Square. He was selling bicycles before Potter and listed himself as a manufacturer. Apart from his main works, there was also a very large workshop on the site of the present Catholic Church in Fore Street, where steam engines and threshing machines were repaired. This business was taken over by Herbert Fiske around 1918, when Shulver moved to Debenham, to establish a Ford dealership there.

Arthur Shulver had his workshop in Well Close Square, where he built the 'Castle' bicycle. His rather bizarre claim was that if you rode one of them, you would prevent broken bones! Other aspects of his trade included the overhaul of steam engines and threshing machines, along with shoeing horses.

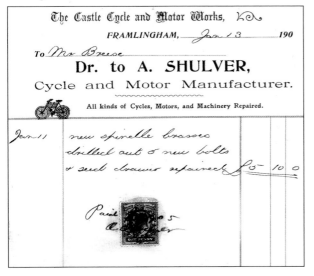

In the late Victorian period, bicycle sales were a way to turn a profit on a relatively high priced article, without significant risk from mechanical breakdown, unlike the new fangled motor car. Dan Scase was selling Rudge Whitworth bicycles from his gun, ammunition and cycle depot on the Market Hill for cash only, from £10. This was still equivalent to about fourteen weeks wages for a horseman at that time, compared with only about one week's pay required to purchase a bike today.

The Plumber, Glazier and Painter

A plumber, from the Latin derivation, was someone who worked with lead, and that would include roofs and weatherproof flashings to walls as well as the more modern association with pipe work. Experience was required in laying a lead roof, as due allowance had to be made for the considerable expansion or contraction caused by extremes of temperature. In a roll joint, the edge of each sheet is dressed over a rounded timber batten so that the overlapped arrangement provided a moving watertight joint. A range of 'sticks', mainly of boxwood, were used to shape the lead. The kitchen sink may have been made of wood lined with lead. The lead pipe could easily be made into a radius bend, but the formation of a T piece involved careful scribing and cutting. By the turn of the century, blow lamps were available, which made the formation of wiped lead joints much quicker.

Many of the larger houses in the town had their own wells in the back garden, capable of a regular supply of cold water. In the late nineteenth century, water for domestic use was provided by three main pumps, one by the river in Albert Place, one in College Road, and the new one at Haynings Corner. This well was sunk in 1897, and a shelter

For a considerable period into the twentieth century, people were still reliant on wells and hand pumps to obtain their daily supply of water. The plumber had to maintain these pumps as the leather washers in particular would need replacement. This excellent photograph should remind us how much we take for granted every time we turn on a tap. The straw and sacking were to protect the pipework from frost damage.

provided, being the gift of the Jeaffreson family. There was no piped supply to houses at this time, but there was work associated with the repair of bellows and washers for private well pumps. In a small town there was unlikely to be sufficient work as a full time plumber, and this trade was often associated with that of the glazier and painter.

George Hunt was a plumber, painter and glazier, with premises in Double Street. His illustrated advertisement of 1890 shows useful details of the plumbing systems available. In order to provide a hot water outlet, it was necessary to have a tank that could supply the cold water make up to the combined heating range and boiler. The tank had to be higher than the taps to achieve sufficient pressure, which could be a problem in a period

George Hunt's advertisement of 1890 shows how water was pumped to a tank to provide the necessary pressure for a hot water supply in a house. The mechanism to the right is a valve operated toilet cistern, without its wooden seat and enclosure.

A. & W. Hunt's bill for pump repairs, 1905.

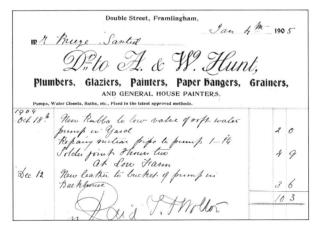

long before the introduction of mains water in 1938. The illustration shows a pipe from the outlet of the handpump to supply such a tank, along with a cold feed and expansion pipe to the range. There would have been a clear responsibility on a member of the domestic staff to ensure the tank was always kept full.

The water closet shown in the same advertisement has a mechanical valve arrangement in connection with the flushing process, which would all have been enclosed with wooden panelling and a seat. These complex arrangements would eventually be replaced by the simple S bend water seal.

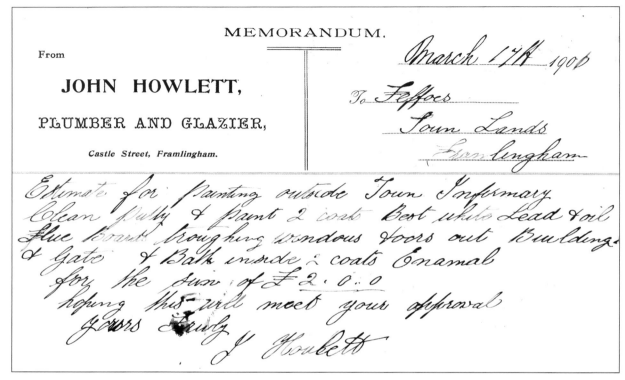

Sewers had been laid in all the streets by 1857, and further improvements made in 1895 with a sewage works costing £3,000. (Note that London did not have its sewers laid until 1865.) Most houses, though, would have relied on an outside toilet, with washing and drinking water provided by bucket from the nearest well. John Howlett of Castle Street was also a plumber, glazier and painter. On his death in 1911, Frank Baldry took over the business.

Paint could be obtained from the ironmonger, who usually also described himself as 'oil and colour merchant'. Reginald Betts the chemist had the same wording in his advertisements. William Barker's stock list of his Market Hill premises for 1892 included prussian blue, spruce ochre, persian red, venetian red, indian red, purple brown, pale ultramarine, raw sienna, burnt sienna and red ochre as dry powders.

The paint was made from these basic pigments combined with a binder and solvent to ease its application. Linseed oil was the commonest binder and drying oil. This was ground with the pigment by hand using a muller (similar to a pestle with a wide base) on a stone slab. Turpentine was the main solvent. This would have been hard work when a substantial quantity was needed. George Sturt entered the family wheelwright business in 1884 and recalled: 'I hadn't strength enough in my arm to grind up Prussian blue for finishing a wagon body'. White lead was the most effective pigment for making white paint, and Barker had five hundredweight of it stocked in kegs. This was a period of change, as other kegs contained various colours that were 'ground in oil'.

We now know that lead in paint and pipework can lead to poisoning. Also, many of the wallpapers were coloured with arsenical preparations. Tom

Tom Dale was a painter and paper hanger as well as a builder. This view of his Market Hill shop shows a number of wallpaper patterns on display in the left hand window, with china and glass in the centre.

Jacob Jay of Station Road, Sudbury, was a plumber, glazier and painter. He also sold the raw materials to other tradesmen.

was made by mixing whiting (chalk powder) to a stiff consistency with water. Colour was added as necessary, along with glue size to prevent it rubbing off.

The glazier would need to order the glass, possibly from a merchant such as George Mason who had a depot at the station until 1904, or a specialist supplier in a larger town. The Crystal Palace of The Great Exhibition in 1851 set a trend by using cylinder glass rather than cast, and this method became prominent in the late Victorian period. This type of glass was made by mouth blowing a cylindrical shape and then cutting off the ends, and along its length. The glass was then reheated and rolled out flat. Machine produced flat glass was not available before about 1920, and it was not until 1959 that the Pilkington Brothers introduced the modern float glass process.

Dale's shop on the Market Hill stocked a range of wallpapers. Expertise is needed for the hanging of paper, especially on the ceiling, and the householder considering such finishes would have employed a tradesman for that work. Graining was a popular finish that could be applied to simulate the effect of wood, while a more basic covering to walls and ceilings was the application of distemper. This was similar to an emulsion finish, and

The trade of plumber, glazier and painter is still very important, and the Victorian tradesman would have adapted well to modern times, although it is likely that he would now only specialise in one area.

Jacob Jay bill for replacing window glass, 1897.

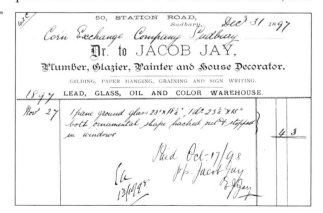

The Printer

This trade was represented in a small way by John Ludbrook and William King in the early part of the nineteenth century, but Richard Green established a business on the Market Hill which became well known in this respect. He had previously been the principal clerk to Charles Clubbe, leading attorney in the town, and was proficient in calligraphy and interested in local history. This culminated in his writing, publishing and printing *The History, Topography and Antiquities of Framlingham and Saxsted* in 1834. By 1851, a young apprentice named Robert Lambert was working for him. After a few years, Green decided to retire from the printing business, but carry on with his book selling and stationery activities in Church Street.

Lambert purchased the printing machinery in 1856, at the age of 21. He applied for a printing press licence in 1859, and produced the first copy of the *Framlingham Weekly News* that year. The paper was initially printed on an iron handpress. Lambert refers to the 'Albion Press', which was a popular make, and had been available from the

1820s, having been developed by Richard Cope in London. It was also used for adverts, posters, notices and general stationery.

The life of a printer in a small business entailed

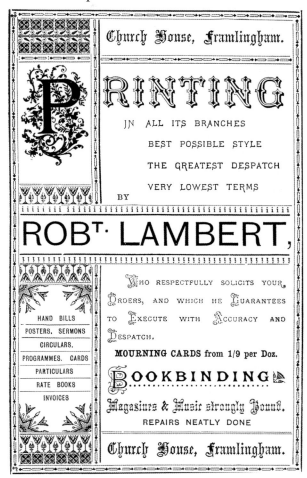

Robert Lambert built up his printing business over 40 years, before selling to James Maulden in 1896. This advertisement illustrates a range of services he provided along with a variety of type faces

long hours and hard work. The letterpress process involved setting the letters onto a composing stick and adjusting the spaces between the words to ensure the margins were aligned ('justifying the line'). The individual lines were then locked into place in a forme or galley. These were then inked by large leather ink pads prior to insertion of the paper into the press and manually applying pressure to produce the printed article. Two people would normally be used for the process, and for the large paper sizes the pressure to be applied was considerable. A manual press with two men could

Interior view of print works (location unknown). The racks, or cases, contain the individual pieces of metal type.

print approximately 250 sheets per hour. The trade was not without its risks: in 1896, John O'Neill had his hand crushed in a printing machine, and part of a finger had to be amputated.

There had been other printers operating in the town. William Dove Freeman ran a printing, stationery and bookselling business in Double Street for many years until his death in 1866. Robert Lambert subsequently bought some of his equipment and moved from Green's Church Street premises into Double Street. In 1871, he employed five people, and after a few years moved to Church House (Regency House).

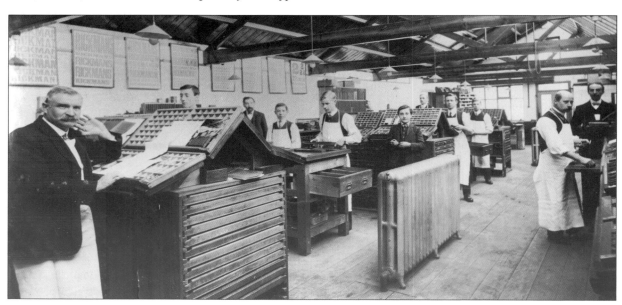

The business was flourishing with the regular *Framlingham Weekly News*, annual production of the *Lamberts Family Almanac*, and revised editions of Green's *Guide* to the town, along with normal commercial printing work. John Self's photographs were used to illustrate the later *Guides*, being printed from half tone blocks produced by White and Limmer of Ipswich.

Maulden's stationery shop in Church Street. The Framlingham Weekly News *and* Lambert's Family Almanac *were printed in the works at the rear. The latter had a print run of 10,000 by the time of Robert Lambert's retirement in 1896.*

The *Almanac* was started in 1857 with a run of 300 copies. When Robert Lambert retired in 1896, the circulation had increased to 10,000, and the printing process had been mechanised. He reminisced in 1907 that 'to such a stage has printing arrived today – miles of paper drawn through cylinder machines, printed and folded without a moment's loss in revolutions!'

James Maulden had built up a successful milling operation in the town, and in 1896 was able to purchase Lambert's printing business, which would be run by his youngest sons Harry and Edwin. By then, much of the laborious work had been reduced by the application of power to the press and they advertised as 'steam printers'. The introduction of steam power enabled rotary presses, which had previously been hand or trea-

A Wharfedale cylinder press by Dawson & Son of Otley near Leeds. The application of steam power to such presses could enable them to print over 1,000 sheets an hour. The Framlingham Weekly News *was produced on this type of press.*

dle operated, to work at a much greater speed. Croppers, Arabs and Wharfedales were equipped with cast iron flywheels and belt driven by a steam

Henry Damant had wide ranging business interests, which included printer, bookseller and insurance agent, as well as running the post and telegraph office.

Post Office, Albert Place, Framlingham.

Mr Jas Breezes

Dr. to HENRY DAMANT,
Printer, ✦ Bookseller ✦ and ✦ Stationer,
∴ *MUSIC SELLER AND BOOKBINDER,* ∴
NEWSPAPER, ADVERTISING AND INSURANCE AGENT.

AGENT FOR THE ALLIANCE FIRE OFFICE.

✦ ✦ Magazines, Music and Books obtained from London Daily. ✦ ✦

1900
Dec. 29 East Anglian   9 9

Paid
Jan 18 1901
H T Damant

H. M. Ives' premises were in King Street, Sudbury, c.1905.

engine. This was the current technology of the late nineteenth century, although it did not improve the quality of the print, only the rate of production. The *Framlingham Weekly News* would eventually be printed on a Double-Demy Wharfedale Press, which was able to produce large printed sheets which were ideal for posters, books and newspapers.

Henry Damant's post office in Albert Place also provided a printing service as part of his stationery business. At the turn of the century there were at least eight people in the town actively involved in printing, being variously described as printer, letterpress printer or compositor.

Although the *Framlingham Weekly News* continued in publication until 1939, in its last year it was printed and published in Lowestoft by the Lowestoft Mercury Co. Ltd. So much local history can pass by unrecorded, and we have to be thankful that the endeavours of Lambert and Maulden have left us with a rich legacy of historical material.

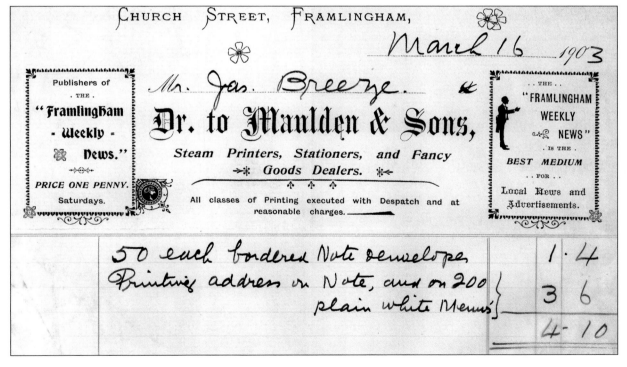

Maulden's bill of 1903 for the supply of notes with printed addresses and menus.

The Railway

The opening of the East Suffolk Railway branch line to Framlingham in 1859 would bring social and economic benefits to the town, which was the motive behind the efforts of John Peirson and others in pursuing it. The earlier means of transporting goods to inland areas were far from efficient, leading to high costs and long delivery times. The railway changed all that. For example, the cost of gas from the town works was reduced as the coal could be bought more cheaply, but the final short journey to the works was still by horse and wagon which limited the benefit.

By the end of the 1800s, commercial development around the station was well established and the goods handled can be gauged from the following returns for 1896:

Passenger tickets	18,349
Coal	8,308 tons
Other freight	25,809 tons

Coal was exclusively incoming along with all manner of goods ordered by shops and individuals. The bulk of outgoing material was corn and agricultural products, while there were pens to hold livestock, which were usually driven there on foot. The opening of the Mid Suffolk Light Railway in 1904 did have an effect on the cattle trade, with the station at Laxfield being only some seven miles away.

E. G. Clarke's business was at the centre of the important barley growing region of England, and as the major brewers expanded, so did the need for good malting barley. Buildings around the station along with additional sidings were provided to handle this trade, which was all moved in sacks at that time. Another important client in terms of volume, if not tonnage, was the Framlingham and District Agricultural Co-operative Society, which by 1912 was handling approximately five million eggs a year, with GER costs of £861.

The railway had operated as the Great Eastern Railway (GER) since 1862, before becoming the London and North Eastern Railway (LNER) in 1923. It is sometimes said that the station should

Goods train number 65467 with crew at Framlingham station. This photo was taken in the 1950s by Dr Allen, who lived in the town and was a great rail enthusiast. To the right of the train in the distance is Clarke's granary, with a bulk wagon visible in the siding.

GER
account
for
transport
of pigs to
Beccles.

| | [695] | G.E.R. FRAMLINGHAM Station 24 . 5 . 1922 No. | | | | | | | | | | | | | | |

Mr J Breese.

Dr. to the GREAT EASTERN RAILWAY COMPANY.

Carriage or other charges are required to be paid on delivery of merchandise unless an account has been opened with the Company.
Cheques and Postal Orders to be made payable to the "GREAT EASTERN RAILWAY COMPANY" and crossed & Co.

Date.	No. of Invoice.	From or To	Sender or Consignee.	No. of articles	Species.	Marks and Numbers.	Weight. Tons cwt. qrs. lbs.	Rate.	Paid on.	Freight. £ s. d.	Cartage or other Charges.	Total. £ s. d.		
	526	Beccles.	24. 5. 22	45	Pigs.		Large.			1 10 6				

Received payment for the Company,

have been more central to the town, but that would have been more restrictive to the goods side which needed plenty of space. Passengers would hardly have been tempted to make a significant journey just because the station was marginally closer, as this was a time when people walked everywhere.

Livestock pens at the station, c.1946. The movement of stock to market had always been an important aspect of the goods traffic on this line, as Framlingham is the centre of a large agricultural region. The opening of the Mid Suffolk Light Railway in 1904 did have an adverse effect on this traffic.

Great Eastern Railway. No. 4
STATION.
WEIGHING MACHINE.
MAR 7 , 1915

From Mr J Breese
To
Species

	TONS.	CWTS.	QRS.		s.	d.
Gross	8	1	2			
Tare	6	18	2			
Nett ...		1	3	0 @		10

Weighing paid
Clerk. [OVER.

Throughout the period 1871 to 1905, Frederick Short was station master and goods manager. The following weekday passenger timetable was operating in the summer of 1900:

Departure	Arrival
7.15 a.m.	7.55 a.m.
8.40 a.m.	11.10 a.m.
12.10 p.m.	12.42 p.m.
4.42 p.m.	5.48 p.m.
7.10 p.m.	8.02 p.m.

The journey time to Wickham Market was 18 minutes, including stops at Parham and Marlesford. Ticket costs in 1900 are shown in the table below. There was a special cattle train that left at 6.10 a.m. on Tuesdays, for the Ipswich market. The charge for a small, medium or large cattle truck was 11s 8d, 13s 11d, and 16s 0d respectively.

A job on the railway was much sought after, as it was usually for life. Reference to the 1901 census shows 20 people were employed in connection with the station. The crossing gates on the line were normally closed to the rail traffic, but the keeper's job was not well paid, and other distractions often resulted in the gates being smashed.

Station buildings were typical of a small terminus, with booking hall, ticket office, master's office, waiting rooms and toilets. There was a single platform, along with a large goods shed, engine shed, coal point and water tower. The increase in motorised road transport in the post war period led to a

Framlingham station in its final period of goods traffic only, late 1950s. The railway provided an important link to the wider world for just over 100 years.

To	1ST CLASS SINGLE	1ST CLASS RETURN	3RD CLASS SINGLE	3RD CLASS RETURN
Wickham Market	1s 3d	1s 10d	6½d	1s 1d
Ipswich	4s 3d	6s 6d	1s 10½d	3s 9d
Liverpool Street	17s 0d	£1 5s 6d	7s 8 d	15s 4d

Horses shunting wagons in the station yard at Long Melford. This was common practice at most country stations, including Framlingham up to the 1920s and Stowmarket as late as 1955.

decline in rail passengers and the last scheduled passenger service was in 1952, with goods traffic continuing until 1965.

The railway was without doubt the single most important factor that increased the commercial prosperity of the town. For just over a hundred years the rail link was maintained, but it finally succumbed to road transport, when the government closed many of the branch lines throughout the country.

COMMERCIAL PROPERTY NEAR THE RAILWAY STATION *(based on the 1904 Ordnance Survey map). The Valuation Office fieldbooks in the National Archives (dating from c. 1912), along with additional local information, give the following information:*

1 *Station Hotel, occupied by F. W. Ablett, owned by Cobbold & Co.*
2 *Coal/corn stroes and steam mill owned and occupied by E. G. Clarke & Son.*
3 *House, granary, stables and coal store occupied by G. E. Symonds, owned by Framlingham & District Agricultural Co-operative Society. (G. E. Mason, builders merchant, occupied the site until 1904. It was subdivided in 1917, when **3A** became Framlingham and Eastern Counties Co-operative Egg and Poultry Society Ltd. and **3B** became The Eastern Counties Farmers' Co-operative Association Ltd.)*
4 *House, granaries, stables, warehouses, coal store, mill, mill house and weighbridge, owned and occupied by Herbert Manby. **4A** was let to the Anglo-American Oil Company Ltd (later Esso) c. 1925.*
5 *Empty granary and stores owned by the executors of T. T. Buckmaster.*
6 *House, warehouse and stable occupied by Pain & Bayles mineral water suppliers; owned by Francis Read.*
7 *Granary and store, plus use of railway siding, occupied by E. G. Clarke & Son; owned by Robert Nesling of Earl Soham.*
8 *Land owned by Nesling, occupied by Clarke & Son and cultivated by Clarke's employees.*
9 *Enclosed land owned by Nesling and used by the Plomesgate RDC for storage purposes.*
Properties 7, 8 and 9, previously owned by James Maulden, were sold at auction in 1906.

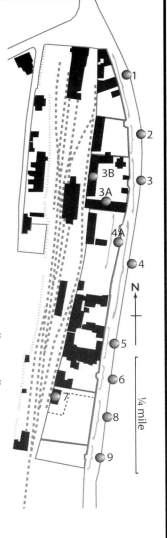

The Saddler

The craft of the saddler, like many others, was an important link in the rural economy, as his work enabled the horse to be harnessed to the wagon or plough. There were three aspects of that work: saddler, harness maker and collar maker.

Brackenbury bill of 1921. The martingale was a strap which was fastened at one end to the nose-band, and to the girth of the horse at the other end.

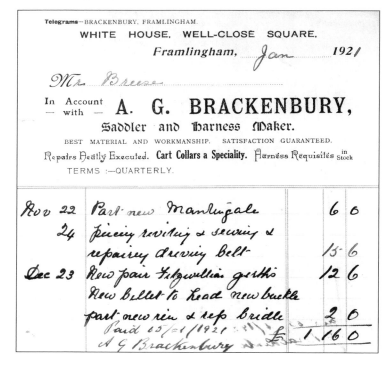

Telegrams—BRACKENBURY, FRAMLINGHAM.

WHITE HOUSE, WELL-CLOSE SQUARE.

Framlingham, *Jan* 192*1*

Mr Breese

In Account — with — **A. G. BRACKENBURY,**

Saddler and Harness Maker.

BEST MATERIAL AND WORKMANSHIP.   SATISFACTION GUARANTEED.

Repairs Neatly Executed.   **Cart Collars a Speciality.**   Harness Requisites in Stock

TERMS :—QUARTERLY.

Nov 22	Part new Martingale	6	0
24	piecing reviting & securing & repairing driving Belt	15	6
Dec 23	New pair Fitzwilliam girths	12	6
	New Billet to Head new buckle part new rein & rep bridle	2	0
	Paid 05/21/1921	£1 16	0
	A G Brackenbury		

Depending on the size of a business, men may have specialised in one branch, or one person might turn his hand to all three. Collar making called for the greatest skill, as each one had to be tailored and made for a specific horse, unlike the saddle which tended to follow a more regular form. Some collar makers would keep a range of sizes in stock, and select the best fit.

Products used for the treatment of leather.

A horse that was ridden or that pulled heavy loads required some form of saddle to spread the weight across its back. The saddle was made from wood, webbing, cloth, leather and wool stuffing. The heavy horse had a more basic cart saddle, over which the ridge chains were located. The saddler would be experienced in all the skills required to make them.

There were various types of harness, but the two main ones were for pulling the cart and the plough. Both had a bridle (dutfin), which incorporated blinkers to limit the horse's field of view, and a bit which passed through the mouth, attached to the reins. The collar holds the wood or metal hames, which form the attachment points for the load to be pulled. The cart harness has additional features in the saddle and breechings, with the latter being leather straps to the rear of the horse to hold back the cart when reversing or going down a hill.

Plough harness does not require the heavy cart saddle, which is replaced by a back and belly band, while the breechings are also not needed. Other forms of harness are the trace, when horses are coupled together in line, and the pair harness for hitching the pole of a dray or similar to a pair of horses. The complexity of the harness had developed over a long period of time, and a visit to a show to see the working horse in action is to be recommended.

The saddlery and harness trade had been long established in Framlingham. George Bloomfield employed several men in the early nineteenth century, with his Well Close Square business passing to George Upton and then William Smith. Job Bridges was also a harness maker on the Market Hill in 1830. By the turn of the century, though, Smith was the only saddler and harness maker in

town. He was to be joined in about 1902 by Solomon Howard, whose Yoxford business was established in 1782. The Howard name for saddlery remained in Framlingham well into the 1960s, when the last craftsmen of that trade emigrated to Australia and made a reputation for camel harness.

The Washbrook saddler Arthur Pearsons at work on a cart saddle. In the background is a nearly completed collar.

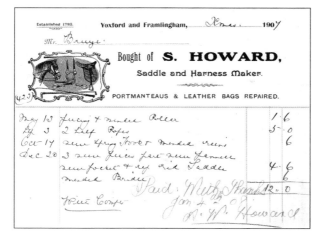

William Smith's bill evokes a slower pace of life than today's. The date is midsummer and accounts are rendered half-yearly.

Solomon Howard had an established business in Yoxford, before opening his shop in Framlingham, c.1902.

There was much hard toil in making a harness. Jack Brackenbury started in the saddlery business with his brother George in 1925, and recalled that a set of driving traces would be about 5 ft 9 inches long, and had to be sewn four times, with eight stitches to the inch. A stitch punch was used to mark the holes, followed by an awl to make the holes and the hand iron to force through the needle. On the heavy horse harness the thread would often make cuts to their fingers, which were plugged with black wax! The harness maker would also stock a range of whips, as each horseman would require two or three, each being of a different type.

Jack specialised in collar making, and like most tradesmen, had his own tools. A long steel rod with notched end, called a stuffing iron, was used to fill the collar, preferably with rye straw. This would then be beaten into shape with a mallet, before packing with flock. Finally, the inner side was lined with a striped collar flannel. Apart from the manufacture of new equipment, there would be a steady call for repairs, as the strains endured by hauling heavy loads were considerable. The manufacture of leather belts for driving farm machinery was also an important sideline for the saddler. Jack's father, Arthur, started his saddlery business around 1910 with Arthur Rooney at the Railway Inn where he was landlord, but later moved to the White House in Well Close Square.

The business eventually passed to Jack and his brother George. The depression in farming meant that money was very tight as most farmers only paid their bills annually. They would collect the harnesses from the farms for repair and try to settle bills at the same time. As the situation worsened, farmers would open accounts with other saddlers to extend their credit, with the hope of better times ahead.

In the 1930s, there was competition in the town, with Howard and Brackenbury on opposite sides of the Square, which occasionally resulted in a spirited exchange over the quality of their work. When times were hard, it was even more necessary to provide a good service at the cheapest price, which would often result in working long hours.

The demise of the working horse often saw the end of this trade when the saddler retired, but some diversified into other aspects of leather craft. George Brackenbury manufactured covers for stacks and farm machinery along with the repair of canvas for the binders, and later on the new combine harvesters.

Arthur Brackenbury started his saddlery business at the Railway Inn, while landlord there. He moved to these premises next to the White House in Well Close Square. Arthur is on the right, with son George to the left, and Rooney Jackson, centre.

The Solicitor

The commercial life of a town was inevitably linked with the need for legal services. The procurement of property, exchange of businesses, seeking redress in the courts, along with the making of wills, all required the services of a solicitor.

In 1830, Framlingham became the centre for the magisterial jurisdiction for all the villages in the Hundreds of Loes, Hoxne, Plomesgate and Thredling. In addition, the County Court was held in the Bridge Street Court House, alternating with Saxmundham every month.

In his day, Charles Clubbe had become a most prominent attorney in the Queen's Bench, and became very wealthy from his practice in

Charles Clubbe became very wealthy from his practice in Framlingham. He died aged 90 in 1876, and was claimed to be the oldest practising solicitor in England.

Framlingham. When he died in 1876 at the age of 90, he was claimed to be the oldest practising solicitor in England. From 1873, the title of attorney was abolished and replaced by that of solicitor, who is an officer of the Supreme Court, appointed by members of the public to act for them.

By the turn of the century there were two firms of solicitors in the town. F. G. Ling had premises on Market Hill and Double Street. Mayhew and Sons also had offices in Double Street and Saxmundham.

The Law Society regulated the profession and, to be admitted, it was necessary to serve a period of training, with a qualified solicitor, which was known as 'articles'. This was for a period of five years, although it had been possible to reduce this to three years provided you were

Richard Lee Mayhew was a solicitor in Saxmundham, and he also had an office in Framlingham, in Double Street.

a BA or LLB from certain universities. The 1901 census shows that Frederick Ling's 16-year-old son Hubert was a solicitor's clerk to be articled, while his older son Gerard was at Cambridge University. Although the profession is looked upon as one that generates considerable income, this was not necessarily the case (as with the medical profession). In the larger towns there were established practices, and it would be hard for a newly qualified solicitor to make a living on his own account. A typical Law Society register of posts in 1902 showed about 50 men advertising for jobs, while only two or three employers were looking for staff. For a market town such as Framlingham, with a large catchment area and only two firms, a comfortable living could be expected.

General information on solicitors' income can be obtained from tax returns of 1913–14. Half the profession had an annual income of £390 or less, and a quarter had less than £185. There were of course many who earned substantially more, but a general view was that £500 was an appropriate income for a solicitor. This was nearly 13 times that of the top farm worker for the same period.

The solicitor's clerk was also in a privileged position, with his knowledge of local business dealings, and arrangements necessary for them. John Martin was a very bright young boy, whose parents were at one time publicans in Needham Market.

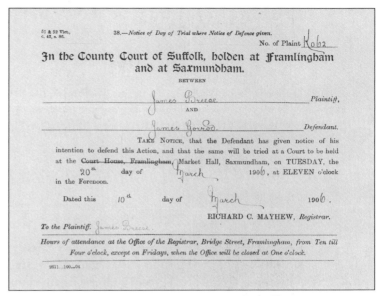

Notice of trial to be held at the Market Hall, Saxmundham, in 1906.

He won school prizes, and by 1865 was employed in Framlingham as the managing clerk to the illustrious Charles Clubbe, at only 17 years of age. He became involved with many activities in the town, taking over the position of clerk to the magistrates on Clubbe's death, and later managing clerk to the County Court, as well as running the Framlingham office of Mayhew and Sons. Office boys might start as early as 12 years of age, before graduating to be engrossing clerks and on to general or managing clerks. In addition to their salary, it was also common for managing clerks to be paid a commission on any business which they found for the practice. John Martin is an example of an ambitious young man who was fortunate to gain a good position.

Mr James Breese
to
I. G. Ling & Son

1914
Dec
1915
Feb

To costs in the purchase by you from Mr I G Barley
of the Church Farm and Mobb's Farm Saxtead for £2700
investigating title preparing conveyances and completing
½ share of the joint costs (say together £21) which
Mr Barley agreed to share equally with you.

10 10 0

Paid
Stamp Duty on Conveyance of Church Farm 20 10 0
"   "   "   "   Mobbs   4 10 0

25 0 0

£ 35 10 0

NB £2 10 0 Stamp Duty will be payable when a
Surrender of the copyhold parts of Church Farm is taken.

LEFT: *Frederick Ling's fee account for legal services in purchasing of Church Farm and Mobbs Farm in Saxtead, 1915.*

By the time of his death in 1904, he had acquired a house in Double Street and College Road, three small farms, and ten cottages. The firm of Ling provided legal services well into the twentieth century from their Church Street office, but Mayhew's presence ceased around the time of World War 1.

Although the courts have long since departed the town, the need for legal services is undiminished and still well represented.

RIGHT: *John Martin started as a managing clerk in Framlingham at the age of 17. He eventually attained the same position in the County Court, became clerk to the Magistrates, and ran the office of Mayhew and Sons from his own house in Double Street.*

The Tanner and Fellmonger

The processing of hides and skins was an integral part of the rural economy, in connection with the disposal of dead animals. Horses that died of old

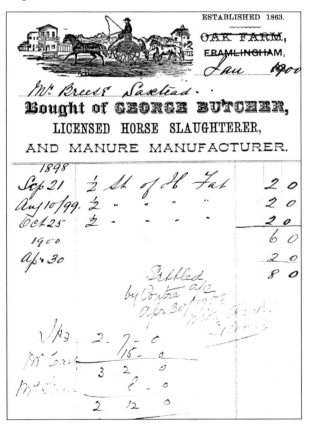

W. George of Elmswell was a horse slaughterer. The traditional form of knacker's cart is evident in this picture.

age, or diseased cattle, all had a value – the hide and skin merchant (the fellmonger) provided a service that would now be known as recycling. By-products could, for example, be converted into fertiliser, glue, grease and leather. He took the skin from a sheep, and separated the wool from it, but it was often the case that the tanner and fellmonger were the same person. Stephen Blumfield carried on both trades in the 1830s, on his premises near the Castle Bridge (next to the Kettleburgh Road junction). He then moved into the town on a site next to the river in Bridge Street. On his death, the business passed to James Clutten and in 1879 to Frank Read. John Edwards, in the early part of the nineteenth century, had a large tannery near the

George Butcher's letterhead, with knacker's cart and dead horse on board. Most parts of an animal were recycled in the form of leather, glue, grease and fertiliser.

old smock mill in Station Road which had a ready supply of spring water from the adjacent pond. That brick lined pond still exists, with the spring providing a constant flow of water. A feature of all tanneries was the considerable number of deep pits required for the various stages of the leather production process. These were often wood lined, or sometimes used brickwork. It was not unusual for the workmen to fall into them, and children were warned by their parents to stay well away from Frank Read's tannery for that reason. These pits were directly fed from the nearby river.

There was an established tannery on this site in Bridge Street (now Tanyard Court) when taken over by Frank Read in 1879. His son Jonathan is on the right. Note the sheepskins, and a ship's figurehead in the garden. In 1921, these buildings were purchased by the Suffolk Electricity Supply Company.

Animal hides would go rotten very quickly, particularly in the summer, and most towns had a tannery so that they could be quickly processed. The main sources of hides were from the butcher as a by-product of his slaughterhouse, and from the fellmonger. It was the tanner who converted them into leather. The first part of that process involved soaking the hides in water, which started the cleaning and also made them absorbent. They were then moved through the lime pits, where the strength of the liquor was increased by adding more quicklime, which helped to loosen the hair, before being removed from the pit and placed over a sloping board. The hide was then scraped with a metal blade to remove the flesh, fat and hair.

The tanning process then began, whereby the hides passed through tanning pits of liquor whose strength was gradually increased. The original liming process was to open up the skins so they would more effectively absorb the tanning liquor. Ground oak bark, which contains tannin, was used for making the liquor, and it was common to see large mounds of bark in the tanner's yard. The tannin penetrates the fibres and displaces the water, the whole process taking up to three months.

The hide would then be trimmed and cut, the thicker butt being formed from the middle section of the back. For harness work, the hide would be cut down the centre in order to achieve a

A feature of all tanneries was the pits filled with liquids required for the various processes. A wet cow hide was very heavy and difficult to remove from the pit. W. & J. Turner, Bramford Road, Ipswich, 1932.

The bowl holds the fat liquor which is brushed over the hide, before it is hung up to dry on tenter hooks or a frame. W. & J. Turner.

greater length. The belts for driving the threshing machines were also made from leather sections, which were jointed by the saddler.

Further processing was necessary after tanning in order to obtain leather that was supple enough for general use, and that was the work of the currier. A hard job, it entailed further washing and scrubbing to get rid of the tanning fluid, along with the use of special knives to level the surface. Finally, the currier worked into the leather a mixture of beef tallow and cod liver oil to provide a smooth, supple material with a great many uses. The Read family embraced this trade, with his mother Elizabeth being a currier, and his son Jonathan a horse slaughterer and fellmonger at the Bridge Street site.

The presence of such a business in the centre of a town would have been a significant source of pollution of the river, as well as the smell in hot weather. Dung was sometimes used to open up the fibre structure of a hide or skin before tanning. This smelly process, when considered along with the arduous work, must have made tanning the least attractive neighbour or occupation.

Improved transport saw the closure of many small tanyards, while larger ones such as Webb and Son of Combs continued into the latter part of the twentieth century, but there are no longer any tanneries in Suffolk.

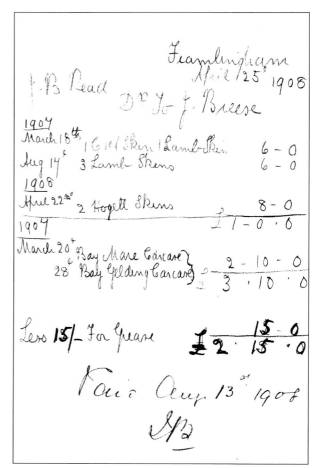

James Breese's bill to Jonathan Read, written on a scrap of paper. Read bought skins and carcases from him which were partly offset by supplying grease, a by-product of the slaughter trade. Another bill of 1907 shows a dead horse to be worth £1 10s 0d.

The Veterinary Surgeon

The welfare for animals on small farms had mainly been provided by the farmer, based on handed down remedies, while the farrier was acknowledged as the person to consult for horse ailments. Even so, White's directory of 1844 lists two veterinary surgeons in Framlingham although in later years one of these 'surgeons' evolved into a farrier.

The Veterinary Surgeons Act of 1881 made it illegal to describe yourself as such unless you had a recognised qualification and were registered

Charles Crickmay Nesling MRCVS *outside his first premises in Well Close Square, c.1895. His brass plaque is displayed on the wall. In 1898, he moved to College Road and ran his practice from the Hermitage.*

84/

FROM Chas. C. Nesling,
Veterinary Surgeon,
Framlingham.

To Mr James Breese
Saxtead

1902

Mar 11th	1 Doz Cough Powders		3 . 6
	Horse measured		- . -
April 13th	Journey Attendance & Medicine to Horse		3 . 6
	½ doz powders left & Medicine to inhale		2 . 6
May 3rd	1 Doz Cough Powders		3 . 6
		£ - . 13 . 0	

Paid Jan 10th /03
Chas Nesling

1902 account for cough powders and attending to a horse.

with the Royal College of Veterinary Surgeons. Charles Nesling from Kenton spent three years at the University of London and qualified in 1889. He started his Framlingham practice in Well Close Square the next year, at the age of 23. Being so young, he grew a beard in order to project an older and wiser image to his clients.

On his marriage in 1898, he bought the Hermitage in College Road where he established his surgery. Farmers would call at any time, and if it were late at night they would enter the surgery and raise the vet via a speaking tube, where the other end was close to his bed in the room above.

A vet's income was mainly from farmers, who usually paid their bills annually after the harvest, and this knock-on effect was evident in most businesses. In larger towns, they were also paid retainers by the main businesses to look after their horses. Charles Nesling was fortunate in also being an inspector for the Ministry of Agriculture, and that work paid more regularly. Another sideline was for the police, who would send him stray dogs to be destroyed. He was paid 6d for this service, with the same amount to his assistant, who also buried the animal. However, his main line of work was with horses, as they were the prime source of power on the farm and for road transport. The castration of colts, docking of tails, dealing with lameness, assisting mares in foaling and general ailments, would have consumed much of his time. Medicines were prepared by the vet from a wide range of ingredients normally stored in a large chest of labelled mahogany drawers.

In a time before the motor car or the telephone system, Charles Nesling travelled extensively in his horse and trap over a wide area. Even when he did have a car, some farms were so difficult to reach that he still used his horse. Being from farming stock, he was interested in all aspects of country life, with his hobby being the breeding and training of heavy-weight hunting horses. In World War 1, he had to visit farms in order to select horses for military use, with the knowledge that many would never return.

Foot and mouth disease is a terrible condition, and was not always stemmed by mass slaughter. Nesling's father was a farmer and cattle dealer and would buy up poorly stock and drive them to Framlingham, where Charles would treat them. They would be released onto the marshy meadows and would eventually recover after a long time, before sale to the local butchers.

The vet was inevitably part of many local organisations, and he was the longest serving secretary of the Framlingham Livestock Association, between 1902 and 1929, along with periods of Honorary Secretary and veterinary officer to the Easton Harriers. Charles Nesling spent his whole working life as a vet in Framlingham, and died there in 1943.

Many owners of livestock would often buy proprietary remedies from the chemist, rather than call in the vet. Reginald Betts described himself as an agricultural chemist, and in 1896 offered:

Condition powders for horses　1s and 2s per tin
Condition balls　3s per dozen
Cough balls　2s per dozen.

These were all made from old recipes of John Betts MRCVS, and had been used by him in his practice for over 50 years. The vet and often the farmer would have a range of instruments available to dispense these medicines. Some horse gags were U-shaped with a central ring that allowed a hand to pass through in order to deliver the dose into the back of the mouth. The ball gun was a tubular device, like a bicycle pump, that held the medicine ball, which was then sent down the throat, without risk of injury to fingers inside the animal's mouth. The blacksmith would have been capable of making various instruments such as teeth rasps, firing irons, and castrating clamps, although by the turn of the century the vet was more likely to purchase these from a specialist supplier. Fleams for blood letting, along with scalpels and saws etc. were kept in velvet lined boxes or leather cases. Chloroform was in use as an anaesthetic, but it was first necessary to control the animal by hobbles or casting ropes. Such work was not without risk, particularly when castrating colts while they were standing! Charles Nesling received a badly fractured arm caused by a horse kicking out.

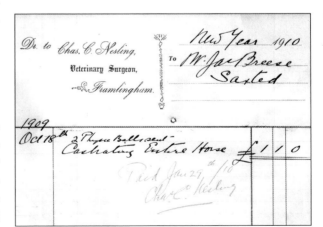

1910 account for castrating a horse.

Appendix I

Directory of commercial information from Kelly's Framlingham 1900

Post, M.O.&T., O.,T.M.O., Express Delivery, Parcel Post, S.B. & Annuity & Insurance Office (Railway Sub-Office). Albert Place – Henry Damant, postmaster. Letters delivered at 7 & 9 a.m. & 6.30 p.m. & dispatched at 12 noon & 8.15 p.m. Box closes at 11.45 a.m. & 8 p.m. Parcels Post delivery closes at 7.45 p.m. Money Orders are granted & paid daily from 8 a.m. to 8 p.m. Telegraph office opens from 8 a.m. to 8 p.m. on week days & 8 to 10 a.m. on Sundays.

Letter Boxes at the Railway Station cleared at 10.40 a.m. & 7 p.m.; College Road, at 7.20 a.m.; Double Street, at 7.10 p.m.; Sundays, 12.20 noon; Dennington Road, at 7.10 p.m.

PUBLIC ESTABLISHMENTS

Cemetery, Fore Street, Charles Lawrie Read, clerk to the Parish Council.

Corn Exchange & Assembly Rooms, Crown Hotel, Market Hill.

County Court, Court House at the Police Station, Bridge Street.

County Police Station, Bridge Street, John R. Lingley, supt. 1 sergeant & 1 constable.

Fire Engine Station, The Castle, 3 manuals & 8 men;

Jonathan B. Read, supt.; George A. Page, sec.

Forester's Hall, Albert Road.

Stamp Office, Henry Damant, Post office.

PUBLIC OFFICERS

Collector of Poor's Rates, Harry Jas. Damant, Albert Place

Collector of Taxes, Thomas Walter Read, Albert Road.

Inland Revenue Officer, Fredk. Wm. Sefton, D'Urbans.

Medical Officer & Public Vaccinator, Framlingham District, Plomesgate Union, Joseph Bowerman Drew L.R.C.P. & S. Edin. The Haynings.

CARRIERS

Robert Scoggins, railway carrier.

W. Meen, to Ipswich, from Crown Hotel, every Thursday.

COMMERCIAL

Adcock, Geo. Rbt. M.R.C.S.Eng., L.R.C.P.Lond. physician & surgeon, medical officer to the Framlingham College, & medical officer & public vaccinator Nos. 4 & 6 districts, Hoxne union & also Framlingham dist. G.E. Rly. Co.

Aldrich Bloom, farmer, Soham Lane

Allen Percy Frederick, butcher, Bridge Street

Balls Frederick William, registrar of births & deaths, relieving & vaccination officer for Framlingham district, Plomesgate Union, Double Street

Barber William, fish merchant, Bridge Street

Barclay & Co. Limited (branch) (Charles Spurrell Kidall, Manager), Market Hill; draw on head office, 54 Lombard Street, London E.C.

Barnes Jane & Mary (Misses), milliners & dress makers, Wellclose Square

Betts Reginald, chemist, Market Hill

Bonney Arthur, baker & confectioner, Albert Place

Borrett Samuel, farm bailiff to Robert Nesling, of Bedfield, Coles Green

Bridges Fruer, blacksmith & agricultural implement agent, Fore Street

Brooks Tom Alfred, Crown family & commercial hotel & posting house

Brownsord John Bryan, butcher, Fore Street

Brunning John, White Horse P.H. Wellclose Square

Buckmaster John, miller (steam & wind) & corn, flour, meal, bran, pollard, malt, hops & coal mer.

Button Frederick, miller (steam) & corn & flour dealer, Station Road

Canham George, pork butcher & shopkeeper, Fore Street

Capon Thomas Morton, farmer

Capon Herbert Meredith, farmer, Red House Farm

Carley Samuel Green & Co. family grocers, & agents for W. & A. Gilbey Lim. Wine & spirit mers. Market Hill

Carr Elizh. (Mrs.), pork butcher & shopkeeper, Market Hill

Catchpole Mary (Mrs.), milliner, Wellclose Square

Catchpole William, chimney sweeper, College Road

Cemetery (Charles Lawrie Read, clerk), Fore Street

Chandler Gibson, farmer, & draining ploughs proprietor & agricultural machinery agent, Saxmundham Road

Clark Henry Stephen, market gardener, Fairfield Road

Clarke Edwin George, maltster & corn, coal & coke mer. Railway Station & Castle Street

Clements Charles, Railway Inn, Woodbridge Road

Clow Mary Ann (Mrs.), Queen's Head P.H. Market Hill

Cocks Walter, wine & spirit merchant, Crown & Anchor La

Coleman Henry, boot & shoe maker, Market Hill

Cone Charles, boot maker, Albert Place

Cook Frederick George, farmer & landowner, Saxtead Rd

Cooke Charles Robert, grocer & provision dlr. Market Hill

Cooper Henry, boot & shoe maker, Castle Street

Corn Exchange & Assembly Rooms, Crown Htl. Market Hill

County Court (Richard Clarkson Mayhew, registrar & high Bailiff)

Crane, Tom, farmer, Badingham Road

Creasy & Co. corn, seed & coal merchants, Railway Station

Creasy Florence (Miss), school for girls, Mount Pleasant

Dale George, stone & marble mason, Bridge Street

Dale Tom, carpenter & glass & china dealer, Market Hill

Damant Harry James, collector of poor's rates, Albert Place

Damant Henry, printer, news agent, bookseller, stationer & stamp distributor, Post office, Albert Place

Dew Arthur, baker, Double Street

Dorling George, grocer, Bridge Street

Downing Charles Edward, rope & twine maker, College Rd

Dowsing Channing P. tailor, Double Street

Drane Henry, fruiterer, Double Street

Drew Joseph Bowerman L.R.C.P.&S.Edin. surgeon, medical officer & public vaccinator, Framlingham district, Plomesgate union, The Haynings

Dring Richard, farmer, Boundary Farm

Durrant Benjamin, butcher, Market Hill

Everson John A. mineral water manufacturer (Charles Fairhead, agent), College Road; & at Harleston, Norfolk

Fairhead Charles, agent to John A. Everson, mineral water manufacturer, College Road

Fairweather John, coal merchant, Wellclose Sq. & Station Rd

Fairweather Henry, gardener & seedsman, Albert Place

Farmers' Club (Charles L. Read, hon. Sec.), held at the Crown Hotel, Market Place

Favell Albert, assistant supt. To the Prudential Assurance Co. Limited, Double Street

Fisk George, draper, Church Street

Fisk John Robert, shopkeeper, Castle Street

Foresters' Hall (Framlingham Castle), Albert Road

Framlingham Association for the Exhibition of Live Stock (John Martin, hon. sec.), Double Street

Framlingham Club & Reading Room (Alfred Mallows, sec.), Station Road

Framlingham College (Rev. Oliver Digby Inskip M.A.,LL.D. head master).

Framlingham Weekly News (Maulden & Sons, publishers; published on Saturday), Church Street

Freeman Wm. China & glass dealer & shoe wareho. Castle St

Freemasons' Lodge (Fidelity, No. 555) (Charles Spurrell Kidall, sec.), held at the Crown Hotel

Fuller James, coal merchant, College Road

Gardner Alice (Mrs.), milliner, Wellclose Square

Gardner E., coal merchant, College Road

Garrard Charles, ironmonger, Market Hill

Garrard Frank Rochfort, farmer & landowner, The Hall

Gas Light & Coke Co. (F.G. Ling, sec.; Charles Garrard, manager), College Road

Gibbs Charles, baker, Fore Street

Girling William, farmer, Brabling Green

Gooch Wyard Trengoe, insurance agent, Castle Street

Goodwin Charles, carpenter & builder, Station Road

Green Robert, hair dresser, Crown & Anchor Lane

Gurneys, Birkbeck, Barclay, Buxtons & Orde, bankers, see Barclay & Co. Limited

Hall George, tailor (repairing), Fore Street

Hammond Walter, shoe maker, College Road

Harmer James, farmer, Cherry Tree Farm

Harvey Edward, fruiterer, College Road

Hawes William, Crown & Anchor family & commercial hotel, Church Street

Heffer Arthur John, beer retailer, Double Street

Heffer James, thatcher, Woodbridge Road

Heffer John, thatcher, Woodbridge Road

Howard John, tailor, Station Road

Howlett John, plumber & glazier, Castle Street

Howlett John, Hare & Hounds P.H., Double Street

Hulland James, chemist & druggist, Market Hill

Hunt A. & W. plumber, glazier & painter, Double Street

Hunt Herbert Edward, boot & shoe maker, Double Street

Hunt Ethel (Miss), fishmonger, Castle Street

Jeaffreson George Cordy L.R.C.P.Lond., M.R.C.S.Eng., L.S.A. surgeon, Market Hill

Jeaffreson George Edwards J.P., M.R.C.S.Eng., L.S.A. surgeon, The Moat house

Jeaffreson John, farmer, Little Lodge Farm

Jude George, general draper & grocer, Market Place

King George, shoe maker & postman, Station Terrace

Lanman Horace Harold, watch maker & dealer in antiques, Bridge Street

Larter Arthur, farmer, Saxmundham Road

Ling Frederic Gaskell, solicitor & commissioner for oaths, & sec. to the Gas Light Company, Market Hill & Double St

Ling William, chimney sweeper, Fore Street

Lingley John R. supt. of police, Police Statn. Bridge St

Mallows Henry & Stephen, builders, Station Road

Mallows Burwood, bricklayer, College Road

Mallows Frank, carpenter, Bridge Street

Mann George,farmer, Great Lodge Farm

Mann Walter, farmer, Countess Wells Farm

Martin John, clerk to the magistrates & managing clerk to the county court, Double Street

Mason George, timber &c. merchant, Railway Station

Maulden & Sons, printers & stationers, Church Street

Maulden James, miller & merchant, roller mills; & at Kelsale mills (wind & steam), Kelsale

Mayhew & Sons, solicitors, Double St., & at Saxmundham

Mayhew Ernest, shopkeeper & coal dealer, College Road

Mayhew Frederick George (firm, Mayhew & Sons), solicitor & commissioner to administer oaths, Double Street; & at Saxmundham

Mayhew Richard Clarkson (firm, Mayhew & Sons), solicitor & commissioner for oaths & perpetual commissioner, Double Street; & at Saxmundham

Middleton Edwin, confectioner, Market Hill

Mobbs Mary Ann (Miss), dress maker, Mount Pleasant

Moore Henry & Charles, wheelwrights, College Road

Moore Charles, carpenter, Bridge Street

Myall Charles, watch maker, Fore Street

Nesling Charles C., M.R.C.V.S. vet. surg. The Hermitage, College Road

Newson Samuel (Mrs.), pork butcher, Bridge Street

Newson Sarah (Miss), dress maker, Fairfield Road

Noble Horace, shopkeeper, College Road

Norman Benjamin (from James Purdeys, London), manufacturer of every description of sporting fire arms, under the patronage of the nobility & gentry of the district, Church Street

Noy William, corn chandler, Castle Street

Odd Fellows' Lodge (Star of the East, No. 2,783), held at the Crown (G.A. Page, sec.)

O'Neill James, drill instructor to the Framlingham College, The Castle

Ostler Jeremiah, cowkeeper, Saxmundham Road

Oxborrow Mary Ann (Mrs.), dress maker, Bridge Street

Oxborrow Robert, boot & shoe maker & greengro. Bridge St

Page Jn. Thomas, brewer & beer retailer, Top of Castle St

Pipe William, farmer, Saxtead Road

Potter Arthur G. basket maker, Station Road

Pratt Frederick (Mrs.), pork butcher, Double Street

Preston Alfd. Auctioneer & house & estate agent, Market Hill

Read Charles Henry & Son, auctioneers & accountants, Albert Road

Read Bessie (Mrs.), milliner, Bridge Street

Read Francis, fellmonger, Bridge Street & currier, Fore St

Read Thomas Waller, collector of taxes, Albert Road

Rivers John, farmer, Earl Soham Lane

Rodwell William & Co. house & business agents & furniture dealers, Double Street

Rose George Edward, farmer, Hatherleigh Farm

Rose James, blacksmith, Wellclose Square

Rudd George Albert, builder, Double Street

Scase Dan, cycle & sewing machine depot, Market Hill

Scoggins Jarvis, furniture broker & general warehouse man, Wellclose Square

Scoggins Robert, carting agent to the G.E. Railway Co., Wellclose Square

Scoggins Albert, farmer, Culpho Farm

Scott James, farmer, Fairfield House, Fairfield Road

Sefton Frederick W. inland revenue officer, D'Urbans

Self John, photographer, Wellclose Square

Self John, tailor, woollen draper, hatter & outfitter, an immense stock always on hand, Wellclose Square

Semmence Brothers, mineral water makers, Castle Street

Shelcott David, farmer, Mount Pleasant

Shulver Arthur, machinist, Wellclose Square

Simmons Mary A. (Mrs.), china, glass & earthenware, Bridge St

Simpson William, confectioner & baker, Wellclose Square

Smith Peter, drain pipe merchant, Woodbridge Road

Smith Peter, jun. brick & tile maker

Smith William, saddler & harness maker, Wellclose Square

Stamp Office (Henry Damant, distributor), Post Office, Albert Pl

Starling Stephen Morell, draper, Market Hill & at Halesworth

Symonds, Joshua, coal merchant, Bridge Street

Taylor, George, farmer, Saxtead Road

Thompson John, farmer, Brabling Green

Thurston Wilfred Warner, hair dresser, Market Hill

Tongman Joseph, poultry breeder, Castle Street

Volunteer Battalion (1st) Suffolk Regiment (G Co. Charles L. Read, commanding)

Vyce James, boot maker, Double Street

Watson Oliver, general dealer, Fairfield Road

Webber Mrs. N. school for ladies, Market Hill

Webster Edward, farmer, Brabling Green

Webster Samuel, farmer, Park Gate Farm

Wells Edward, tailor & woollen draper, Market Hill

White Alfred James, watch maker, Albert Place

Wightman John, carpenter, Double Street

Wolton Plant, farmer & cattle dealer, Fore Street

Woodward James, Station commercial hotel & posting house, Woodbridge Road

Wright Thomas James, music seller, Wellclose Square

Appendix 2

Population change in Suffolk towns

	1801	1851	1901	1801–1901
Beccles	2,788	4,398	6,898	+147%
Bungay	2,439	3,841	3,314	+ 36%
Eye	1,734	2,587	2,004	+ 16%
Framlingham	1,854	2,450	2,526	+ 36%
Hadleigh	2,332	3,716	3,245	+ 39%
Halesworth	1,676	2,662	2,246	+ 34%
Haverhill	1,308	2,535	4,862	+272%
Leiston	823	1,580	3,259	+296%
Mildenhall	2,283	4,374	3,567	+ 56%
Newmarket	1,792	3,356	6,874	+284%
Saxmundham	855	1,180	1,452	+ 70%
Stowmarket	1,761	3,306	4,162	+136%
Stradbroke	1,215	1,822	1,016	– 16%
Sudbury	3,283	5,225	6,421	+ 96%

Framlingham census figures

1801	*1,854*
1811	*1,965*
1821	*2,327*
1831	*2,445*
1841	*2,523*
1851	*2,450*
1861	*2,252*
1871	*2,569*
1881	*2,518*
1891	*2,525*
1901	*2,526*
1911	*2,400*
1921	*2,397*
1931	*2,101*
1941	*No census*
1951	*1,943*
1961	*2,005*
1971	*2,230*
1981	*2,190*
1991	*2,941*
2001	*3,114*

Appendix 3

1901 Framlingham census: commercial trades and professions

W= Worker, E = Employer, OA = Own Account (i.e. self-employed)

	W	E	OA
Agriculture (21.4%)			
Farmer		18	7
Farmer's son	10		
Bailiff	7		
Poultry/pig farmer	2		
Agricultural machine proprietor		1	
Cattle dealer			1
Horseman	35		
Carter on farm	4		
Farm labourer	79		
Gamekeeper	1		
Hay cutter	3	1	
Milk boy	1		
Shepherd	2		
Stockman/boy	28		
Apartment letting (0.1%)			1
Auctioneer's clerk (0.1%)		1	

	W	E	OA
Baker and confectioner (1.5%)			
Baker	1		3
Confectioner		1	
Baker and confectioner			2
Assistants etc.	7		
Banking (0.2%)			
Manager	1		
Clerk	1		
Basket maker (0.2%)			
Maker	1		
Apprentice	1		
Bicycles (0.4%)			
Manufacturer			1
Assistant, apprentice	3		
Blacksmith (1.5%)			
Blacksmith	9	2	2
Boiler maker riveter	1		

	W	E	OA
Boots and shoes (2.5%)			
Boot/shoe maker	6	2	12
Assistant, apprentice	4		
Building (3.2%)			
Builder		4	
Bricklayer	12		
Bricklayer's labourer	4		
Brick, tile maker	4	1	
Brick, tile maker's labourer	3		
Stonemason	2		1
Carpenter and wheelwright (2.8%)			
Carpenter, joiner	15	1	1
Carpenter's assistant/apprentice	2		
Cabinet maker	1		1
Wheelwright	2	2	
Wheelwright's apprentice	1		
Chemist, druggist (0.2%)		2	
Chimney sweep (0.2%)			2
Coal (1.9%)			
Coal merchant	2	2	5
Labourer	3		
Carter	5		
Miner	1		
Corn (2.8%)			
Corn merchant	3	4	1
Clerks, travellers, labourers, porters	15		
Carter	4		

	W	E	OA
Doctor (0.4%)			4
Domestic service (25.3%)			
Charwoman	11		
Coachman	3		
Cook	14		
Errand boy/girl	7		
General servant, help, domestic, housekeeper, companion etc.	155		1
Groom, ostler	14		
Laundress	11		11
Nurse	15		1
Draper and outfitter (10%)			
Draper		2	2
Draper's assistant/apprentice	20		
Dressmaker	21	1	18
Dressmaker's assistant/apprentice	4		
Milliner	1		4
Milliner's apprentice	1		
Tailor	13	3	4
Tailor's assistant/cutter	2		
Excise officer (0.1%)	1		
Fishmonger (0.3%)	1	1	1
Florist and gardener (0.3%)	1	1	1
Engine driver (0.4%) (for mill and bacon factory)	4		
Fruiterer (0.1%)			1
Furniture dealer (0.1%)			1

	W	E	OA
Grocer (2.4%)			
Grocer		4	2
Assistant, salesman, porter	17		
Gunsmith (0.2%)	1		1
Hairdresser (0.2%)			2
Harness maker (0.2%)	2		
Hawker (0.3%)	1		2
Insurance agent (0.3%)	3		
Ironmonger (1.0%)			
Ironmonger		1	1
Assistant, porter	5		
Whitesmith, tinsmith	1		2
Labourers, general (4.1%)			
Gardener	14		1
Gas stoker	1		
General labourer	17		
Road labourer	5		
Timber yard labourer	1		
Land agent (0.1%)			1
Machine mender (0.2%)	2		
Malting (0.7%)			
Maltster	3		
Carter	1		
Labourer	2		
Traveller	1		
Mechanical dentist (0.1%)			1

	W	E	OA
Milkman (0.2%)			2
Milling (2.1%)			
Miller	6	2	
Millstone dresser	2		
Apprentice	2		
Carter	8		
Mineral water manuf. (0.2%)	1	1	
Photographer (0.1%)			1
Plumber, glazier, painter (0.5%)			
Painter	2		
Plumber		1	
Plumber and glazier			1
Plumber and painter		1	
Post Office (0.8%)			
Sub postmaster	2		
Post Office assistant	4		
Postman	4		
Telegraph messenger	1		
Printer (1.0%)			
Printer, compositor	5	2	
Stationer's apprentice	3		
Public House etc. (2.6%)			
Innkeeper, licensed victualler, hotel proprietor		2	6
Barman, cellar, clerk, porter	12		
Beerhouse keeper			1
Brewer		1	

	W	E	OA
Brewer's clerk, porter	2		
Wine merchant		1	

Railway (2.1%)

	W	E	OA
Station manager	1		
Acting fireman	2		
Booking clerk	1		
Carter	1	1	
Engine driver	2		
Gatehouse keeper	1		
Guard	1		
Platelayer	3		
Porter	5		
Shunter	1		
Signalman	1		

Rate collector (0.1%) — W: 1

Rope manufacturer (0.1%) — OA: 1

Singer sewing machine agent (0.1%) — 1

Tanner, fellmonger (0.4%)

	W	E	OA
Fellmonger	1	1	
Tan yard labourer	2		

Thatcher (0.3%) — W: 1, E: 1, OA: 1

Valuation and relieving officer, registrar of births/deaths (0.1%) — 1

Veterinary surgeon (0.1%) — E: 1

Watchmaker, jeweller (0.5%)

	W	E	OA
Watchmaker, jeweller	1	1	2
Assistant	1		

	W	E	OA
TOTAL	**755**	**75**	**130**

Note: The above figures exclude people employed in education, the church and the police force.

MAJOR EMPLOYMENT TYPES

Domestic service	25.3%	Corn	2.8%	Coal	1.9%
Agriculture	21.4%	Publican	2.8%	Butcher	1.7%
Draper, outfitter	10.0%	Boots and shoes	2.6%	Baker, confectioner	1.5%
General labourer	4.1%	Grocery	2.5%	Blacksmith	1.5%
Building	3.2%	Milling	2.4%	Printer	1.0%
Carpenter, wheelwright	2.8%	Railway	2.1%	Ironmonger	1.0%

All percentage values are in relation to the total work force considered.

Appendix 4

Framlingham telephone numbers

Based on the 1923 directory, along with some numbers determined from early accounts.

1 Post Office, Bridge Street
2 Barclays Bank, Market Hill
3 Carley and Co., Market Hill, grocer
4 Clarke E. G., maltster, corn, coal merchant
5 Baldry Frank, builder
6 Framlingham and Eastern Counties Co-op. Egg and Poultry Society Ltd., Station Road
7 Garrard Charles, ironmonger etc., Market Hill and Fore Street
8 Larter John, livestock agent and farmer, Cherry Tree Farm
9 Ling F. G. and Son, solicitors, Church Street
10 Manby and Co., corn, seed and coal merchant, Station Road
11 Garrard P. B., farmer, Framlingham Hall
12 Police Station, Bridge Street
13 Woodgate William, farmer, breeder and exporter of Suffolk horses, Suffolk sheep and pigs, Red Poll cattle, Fairfield House
14 Wicks A. T., drapers, milliners etc., London House, Market Hill

15 Potter A. G., motor engineers and agricultural tractor specialists, Station Road and Market Hill
16 Lloyds Bank, Market Hill
17 Goodwin Charles, East View
18 Allen Percy, butcher, Bridge Street
19 Baldry Frank, Hill Crest, Pembroke Road
20 Armstrong C. W., physician, Pembroke Lodge
21 The International Tea Company's Stores Ltd., Bridge Street
22 Crown Hotel, Market Hill
23 Reade Mrs, Aldehurst
24 Larter Isaac, farmer, Hatherleigh House and Moat Farm
25 Capon H., Dennington Hall/Manby H., Dennington Lodge
26 Eye Division Conservative and Unionist Association
27 Hunter Sidney, White House Farm, Parham
28 Clarke Hugh, Saxtead Lodge
29 Framlingham College
30 Eastern Counties Farmers Co-operative Association, Station Road

Appendix 5

Conversions

Currency

(Decimal currency was introduced in 1971, when the pound became 100 new pence instead of 240 old pence.)

OLD		NEW
1 guinea	=	£1.05
20 shillings	=	£1.00
1 pound (£1)	=	£1.00
1 crown	=	25 pence
half a crown	=	12.5 pence
1 florin	=	10 pence
1 shilling (*s*)	=	5 pence
1 penny (*d*)	=	0.42 pence

Length

OLD		NEW
1 inch	=	25.4 mm
1 foot	=	304.8 mm
1 yard	=	914.4 mm
1 mile	=	1.61 km
1 rod	=	5.03 m

(The rod, pole and perch are the same unit of length.)

Volume

Old		New
1 pint	=	0.57 litre
1 gallon	=	4.55 litres
1 peck	=	9.09 litres
1 bushel	=	36.37 litres
1 coomb	=	145.48 litres
1 quarter	=	290.95 litres

Mass

1 ounce	=	28.35 g
1 pound	=	0.45 kg
1 stone	=	6.35 kg
1 cwt (hundredweight)		
	=	50.8 kg
1 ton	=	1016.06 kg

Barrel sizes

1 pin	=	20.46 litres
1 firkin	=	40.91 litres
1 kilderkin	=	81.83 litres
1 barrel	=	163.66 litres

Coomb sack weights

wheat	=	110 kg
barley	=	100 kg
beans	=	120 kg
flour	=	127 kg

Area

Old		New
1 acre	=	4046.86 m²
1 rood	=	1011.71 m²

Velocity

1 mile per hour = 1.61 km/hour

Temperature

$$°F = (°C \times 1.8) + 32$$

Appendix 6

Places to visit

The following is a select list of places that have information and exhibits relevant to the subject matter of this book. Always check opening times before visiting.

Beccles and District Museum
Leman House, Ballygate, Beccles
Tel: 01502 715722
www.becclesmuseum.org.uk

Buttrum's Mill
Burkitt Road, Woodbridge
Restored six- storey tower mill.
Tel: 01473 583352
www.visit-woodbridge.co.uk

East Anglia Transport Museum
Chapel Road, Carlton Colville, Lowestoft
Tel: 01502 518459
www.eatm.org.uk

Easton Farm Park
Easton
Tel: 01728 746475
www.eastonfarmpark.co.uk

Felixstowe Museum
Viewpoint Road, Felixstowe
Tel: 01394 674355
www.felixstowe-museum.co.uk

Greene King Museum
Westgate Brewery, Bury St Edmunds
Tel: 01284 714382
www.greeneking.co.uk

Ipswich Transport Museum
Cobham Road, Ipswich
Tel: 01473 715666
www.ipswichtransportmuseum.co.uk

Lanman Museum
Framlingham Castle, Framlingham
Tel: 01728 723214
www.framlingham.com

Long Shop Museum
Leiston
Tel: 01728 832189
www.longshop.care4free.net

Mid Suffolk Light Railway Museum
Brockford Station, Wetheringsett
Tel: 01449 766899
www.mslr.org.uk

Museum of East Anglian Life
Stowmarket
Tel: 01449 612229
www.eastanglianlife.org.uk

Pakenham Water Mill
Mill Road, Pakenham
Tel: 01359 230269 or 01787 247179
www.pakenhamwatermill.co.uk

Saxtead Post Mill
Saxtead, near Framlingham
Tel: 01728 685789
www.english-heritage.org.uk

The Suffolk Punch Heavy Horse Museum
The Market Hill, Woodbridge
Tel: 01394 380643
www.suffolkhorsesociety.org.uk

William Clowes Museum of Print
Newgate, Beccles
Tel: 01502 712884
www.clowes.co.uk

Further Afield

Amberley Working Museum
Houghton Bridge, Amberley, Arundel, West Sussex
Tel: 01798 831370
www.amberleymuseum.co.uk

Beamish, The North of England Open Air Museum
County Durham
Tel: 01207 231811
www.beamish.org.uk

The Black Country Living Museum
Tipton Road, Dudley, West Midlands
Tel: 0121 557 9643
www.bclm.co.uk

Coors Visitor Centre and Museum of Brewing
(former Bass Museum)
Horninglow Street, Burton on Trent
Tel: 0845 6000 598
www.bass-museum.com

Cambridge Museum of Technology
Cheddars Lane, Cambridge
Tel: 01223 368650
www.museumoftechnology.com

The Connected Earth Museum on the Internet
www.connected-earth.com

The Fakenham Museum of Gas and Local History
Hempton Road, Fakenham, Norfolk
Tel: 01328 863150
www.northnorfolk.org/fakenhammuseum

Forncett Industrial Steam Museum
Low Road, Forncett St Mary, Norwich
Tel: 01508 418277
http://oldenginehouse.users.btopenworld.com/
Forncett.htm

Gunton Park Sawmill
Gunton Park, Hanworth, Norwich
Tel: 01603 222705
www.norfolkwindmills.co.uk

Museum of Power
Steam Pumping Station, Hatfield Road, Langford,
Maldon, Essex
Tel: 01621 843183
www.museumofpower.org.uk

Science Museum
Exhibition Road, London
Tel: 0207 942 4000
www.sciencemuseum.org.uk

Bibliography

The following books can provide further information on specific areas of interest:

Maurice Baren, *Victorian Shopping* (London: Michael O'Mara Books, 1998).

Jack Brackenbury, *Jack's Story* (1995). Covers his early life in Framlingham.

John Bridges, *Early Country Motoring: Cars and Motorcycles in Suffolk 1896–1940* (Little Waldingfield: J. F. Bridges, 1995).

John Bridges, *Framlingham: Portrait of a Suffolk Town* (Long Melford: J. F. Bridges, 1975).

C. R. Bristow, *A Directory of Nineteenth and Twentieth Century Suffolk Breweries* (Ipswich: Salient Press, 1985).

Jonathan Brown, *The English Market Town* (Marlborough: Crowood Press, 1986).

Christine Clark, *The British Malting Industry since 1830* (London: Hambledon Press, 1998).

Phyllis Cockburn, *Whitmore and Binyon, Engineers and Millwrights of Wickham Market, Suffolk* (2005).

Ashley Cooper, *Our Mother Earth: Of the Furrow Born* (Bulmer: Bulmer Historical Society, 1998).

Anne Digby, *The Evolution of British General Practice 1850–1948* (Oxford: Oxford University Press, 1999).

George Ewart Evans, *Ask the Fellows Who Cut the Hay* (London: Faber, 1956)

George Ewart Evans, *The Horse in the Furrow* (London: Faber, 1960).

George Ewart Evans, *The Pattern Under The Plough* (London: Faber, 1966).

George Ewart Evans, *The Farm and The Village* (London: Faber, 1969).

George Ewart Evans, *Where Beards Wag All* (London: Faber, 1970)

George Ewart Evans, *The Days That We Have Seen* (London: Faber, 1975).

George Ewart Evans, *From Mouths of Men* (London: Faber, 1976).

George Ewart Evans, *Horse Power and Magic* (London: Faber, 1979).

Brian Flint, *Suffolk Windmills* (Woodbridge: Boydell Press, 1979).

John Geraint Jenkins, *The English Farm Wagon: Origins and Structure* (Lingfield: Oakwood Press, 1961).

John Hewitt, *Two Horse Power* (Lavenham: Terence Dalton, 1991).

David Hey, *How Our Ancestors Lived: A History of Life a Hundred Years Ago* (Richmond: Public Record Office, 2002).

Allan Jobson, *Household and Country Crafts* (London: Elek, 1953).

J. L. Kieve, *Electric Telegraph: A Social and Economic History* (Newton Abbot: David and Charles, 1973).

Harry Kirk, *Portrait of a Profession: A History of the Solicitor's Profession 1100 to the Present Day* (London: Oyez Publishing, 1976).

Robert Malster, *Suffolk At Work* (Stroud: Sutton, 1995) (Britain in Old Photographs series).

John McEwan, *Lambert's Framlingham, 1871–1916* (2000).

G. E. Mingay, *Rural Life in Victorian England* (London: Heinemann, 1977).

Robert Pearce, *Britain: Society, Economy and Industrial Relations 1900–39* (London: Hodder and Stoughton Educational, 2002).

David Pitcher, *All Change for Framlingham* (2002).

Harold Preston, *Early East Anglian Banks and Bankers* (Thetford: H. Preston, 1994).

Henry Rider Haggard, *A Farmer's Year: Being his Commonplace Book for 1898* (London: Longmans, 1899).

Walter Rose, *The Village Carpenter* (Wakefield: E.P. Publishing, 1973).

Oswald Sitwell, *Framlingham: a Short History and Guide* (Framlingham: Ancient House, 1974).

Norman Smedley, *East Anglian Crafts* (London: Batsford, 1977).

Norman Smedley, *Life and Tradition in Suffolk and North-East Essex* (London: Dent, 1976).

George Sturt, *The Wheelwright's Shop* (Cambridge: Cambridge University Press, 1923).

Rex Wailes, *The English Windmill* (London: Routledge & Kegan Paul, 1954).

Colin Waters, *A Dictionary of Old Trades, Titles and Occupations* (Newbury: Countryside Books, 1999).

Shire Publications also produce many useful titles including: *Bricks and Brickmaking, Brewing and Breweries, Corn Milling, Gas Lighting, Shoemaking, The Victorian Chemist and Druggist, Domestic Servant, Ironmonger, Public House, Printer, The Village Blacksmith.*

Video: *Bygones, Gone to Burton* (Ipswich: Old Pond Publishing)

Location map

1 Sale yard
2 Alfred Preston (auctioneer)
3 Crown Hotel/Corn Exchange
4 Simpson (baker)
5 Bonney (baker)
6 Middleton (confectioner)/Holmes (baker)
7 Edwards/Carley (grocer)
8 Barclays (bank)
9 Lloyds (bank)/Dr Jeaffreson
10 Bridges (blacksmith) c. 1724
11 Bridges (blacksmith) from 1820s
12 Rose/Girling/Fairhead (blacksmiths)
13 Coleman (bootmaker)
14 Cone/Self (bootmaker)
15 Castle brewery / inn
16 Haynings (maltings)
17 Maulden (maltings and mill)
18 Crown and Anchor
19 Nesling (veterinary surgeon)
20 Farrier's Arms
21 Hare and Hounds
22 Queen's Head
23 Railway Inn

24 White Horse
25 Mayhew (solicitor)
26 Mallows (builder)
27 Brownsord/Durrant (butcher)
28 Allen (butcher)
29 Moore (wheelwright)
30 Dale (builder/carpenter)
31 Hulland/Garrod (chemist)
32 Betts/Gostling/Sara/Stevens (chemist)
33 Green (telegraph/post office), Cooke (grocer)
34 Damant (telegraph/post office)
35 Post Office/telephone exchange
36 Telephone exchange from 1926
37 Ling (solicitor) after WW1
38 Self (tailor)
39 Garrard/Jude/Barnes/Ady/Wareing (draper etc.). Potter (from 1930)
40 Starling/Wicks (draper etc.)
41 Dowsing (tailor)
42 Fisk/Freeman (outfitter)
43 Barker/Garrard (ironmonger)
44 Tannery/electricity works

45 Gas works
46 Courthouse
47 Dorling (grocer)
48 International Stores (grocery)
49 Cooper (tailor)
50 Norman (gunsmith and sports)
51 Scase (gunsmith and sports)
52 Autey (ironmonger)
53 Scoggins (general dealer)
54 United Reformed Church (originally steam mill)
55 Button (steam mill; approx. location)
56 Potter (old Reading Room)
57 Potter (shop)
58 Walne (garage)
59 Shulver/ Fiske (cycle dealer)
60 Lambert/Maulden (printer)
61 Howard (saddler)
62 Brackenbury (saddler)
63 Brooke Keer (maltings)/Garrard (garage)
64 Moore (barber)
65 Baldry (builder)
66 Kerridge (butcher)
67 Read (milliner)

N

Meres

Castle

Church

COLLEGE ROAD

NEW ROAD

BRIDGE STREET

WELLCLOSE SQUARE

MARKET HILL

CHURCH STREET

CASTLE STREET

DOUBLE STREET

ALBERT PLACE

ALBERT ROAD

STATION ROAD

BROOK LANE

FORE STREET

FAIRFIELD ROAD

½ mile

Framlingham,
based on the 1904
Ordnance Survey map

Index

Interior view of the Hare and Hounds in the 1980s by John Western. Jimmy Finbow the landlord is behind the counter.

Monewden wheelwright's shop. This 1988 watercolour by John Western shows the interior then, but it would not have changed much since the turn of the century. Note the patterns for the felloes hanging from the wall, along with augers, braces, cramps, leg vices and much more.